LEADERSHIP
LESSONS
From The
PUB

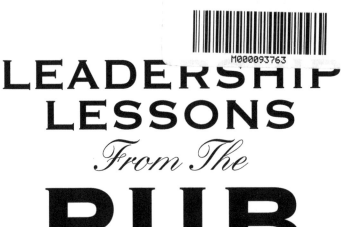

HARNESSING THE POWER OF EMOTIONAL INTELLIGENCE TO BUILD A FULLY ENGAGED WORKPLACE

IRVINE NUGENT

INDIE BOOKS
INTERNATIONAL

ISBN: 978-1-952233-33-3
Library of Congress Control Number: 2020921695

Designed by Joni McPherson, mcphersongraphics.com

INDIE BOOKS INTERNATIONAL, INC®
2424 VISTA WAY, SUITE 316
OCEANSIDE, CA 92054
www.indiebooksintl.com

Cover Photo: Kirwan's Pub, Washington, DC, www.kirwansonthewharf.com

To my parents, Brian and Teresa, my husband, Fred, and my sisters, Susan, Ann, Catherine, and Mary, who have always been a font of love and support for me.

CONTENTS

TABLE OF FIGURES

Figure 6.3 The snug in Doheny & Nesbitt Pub, Dublin, Ireland. Photo courtesy of Dublin Snugs.

Figure 7.1 Carrick-a-Rede island and its famous rope bridge. Photo courtesy of Phb.cz / Deposit Photos Stock Photo.

Figure 7.2 Looking down from the Carrick-a-Rede rope bridge. Photo courtesy of pgabophotos / Deposit Photos Stock Photo.

Figure 7.3 A section of the peace wall dividing communities. Photo courtesy of Luc De Zeeuw, https://www.flickr.com/photos/luc-de-zeeuw/.
Figure 7.4 TKI Profile Model

Figure 8.1 Strabane Chronicle Newspaper ad for upcoming Ballymagorry Arms entertainment. Photo courtesy of Irvine Nugent.

Figure 9.1 Kevin and myself somewhere in the Dublin mountains. Photo courtesy of Irvine Nugent.

Figure 9.2 A view of the early monastic ruins in Glendalough. Photo courtesy of Irvine Nugent.

Figure 9.3 The Korean War Memorial. Photo courtesy of Irvine Nugent.

PREFACE

R
ight now, ladies and gents, could you please finish up your drinks?" The fifteen remaining customers looked at me, smiled, and did not budge. "Right now, ladies and gents, could you please finish up your drinks?" I said in a louder voice, just on the off-chance they had not heard me the first time. Again, not a budge. "Right now, ladies and gents, do you not have any homes to go to?"

With a smile on his face, John, a regular at the pub replied, "Aw, wee Irvine, if you knew what was waiting for me at home, sure, you would be giving me another drink and not throwing me out." And so, the nightly negotiation of trying to empty the pub at closing time had begun.

Thirty years later, I found myself leading an organization with over 450 employees. In that role, I was responsible for setting out a vision, managing a difficult change initiative, dealing with conflict, negotiating new contracts, trying to influence outside stakeholders, managing difficult employees, and remaining calm even when emotionally triggered. As I struggled to combat all these demands, I found myself, more often than not, going back to the pub to mine some nuggets of wisdom I'd learned from my parents.

This book was born out of that unique Irish wisdom. In addition, this book comes from countless hours of listening to leaders' coaching sessions as they talked through issues with which they were struggling. In working with these leaders, I have seen that most, if not all, of our struggles are initially answered by going inward and exploring our emotional intelligence. This book journeys through Ireland's rich pub culture and back to the boardrooms and offices of the organizations you lead or manage. It's a journey into the struggle of leadership that keeps this famous Irish saying in mind: Wisdom is the comb given to a man after he has lost his hair.

Irvine Nugent
September, 2020

CHAPTER 1

Watch Me Build Again

Friday, March 30, 1973, was a perfect spring day in the sleepy Northern Irish village of Ballymagorry. As the sun began to set, the only noise came from the village's only pub, Ballymagorry Arms. Little did anyone know the horrors that were in store.

The pub's owners, Brian and Teresa, were just returning from a shopping trip in Belfast. Teresa immediately went upstairs above the pub where their family lived. She was excited to show her daughters—Susan, Ann, Kate, and Mary—a new dress she had purchased to wear to the wedding of her sister-in-law, Maureen. Brian was anxious to get into the pub and relieve the bartender who had been working all day.

An hour later, two masked Irish Republican Army (IRA) gunmen stormed into the pub. One of them gathered all the customers and held them at gunpoint against the wall. The other went to the counter, placed a firebomb on top of it, and lit the fuse.

The gunman looked at Brian and said, "You've five minutes to clear the place before this goes off. If any of ye tries to move it, it'll explode."

After the gunmen left, the customers fled out the front doors. Brian ran up the back stairs to warn Teresa and their daughters, who were still chatting in the living room. Finally, he ran to the bedroom of his sleeping six-year-old son. Brian grabbed his son from the bed, ran out the bedroom door, down the stairs, out the side door, and across the street. He was relieved to see Teresa and his daughters had already made it outside safely.

Just then, an explosion so terrible and powerful erupted and the roof lifted from the building. Fire instantaneously spread throughout the pub and home. Brian, Teresa, and their children watched as everything they owned went up in flames before their very eyes. Still clinging tightly to his son, Brian raised a clenched fist in defiance and from deep within himself he cried, "Watch me build again."

Brian was my father and I still remember that clenched fist.

Figure 1.1. The remains of Ballymagorry Arms after the 1973 bombing.

Figure 1.2. The front of Ballymagorry Arms a day after the bombing. The burnt-out window upstairs on the left was my bedroom.

In Northern Ireland in 1973, "The Troubles" entered a new, more dangerous phase. Between 1969 and 1998, the world watched in horror as this beautiful and charming land was torn apart by violence that bordered, at times, on civil war; this conflict was euphemistically called The Troubles. These troubles had been brewing for many decades, if not centuries. The 1960s saw mounting civil rights demonstrations demanding an end to discrimination against the Catholic and Nationalist minority population by the Protestant and Unionist majority.

This conflict was inspired by the civil rights movement in the United States.[1] Indeed, during the marches in Northern Ireland at this time, you could hear protestors sing the gospel song, "We Shall Overcome," the cornerstone of every American civil rights march and protest. Toward the end of the 1960s, the protests gained a violent, deadly face with the rise in paramilitary groups from each side of the sectarian divide. On the nationalist side—the IRA; on the unionist side—the UVF (Ulster Volunteer Force).

For a few days after that terrible pub bombing, my mother disappeared. We later learned that she had been pregnant with her sixth child but miscarried due the acute stress of the bombing. My sisters and I had been placed in different neighbors' homes until we found new accommodations. Each of us dealt with the situation in our own unique ways.

For me, the tragedy brought a wave of popularity at school. The bombing had been on the BBC news and it was all anyone could talk about in the village and at school. When I went back to class, I was the star attraction. We had been on television and I was the most famous six-year-old in school.

My father, however, found a spark deep within that inspired him to keep his promise of rebuilding the pub. Yes, it would have been easy for him to burn with anger and seek revenge, or to curl up and declare defeat, but he chose to rebuild. With great calm, he began to act in the days after the bombing. He arranged to have a tent delivered and set it up in the parking lot at the side of the pub and got a new shipment of drinks. People from the village brought chairs and tables and tried to help in whatever way they could, inspired by my father's quiet resolve.

Friday, April 6, just one week after the bombing, was a magical day. On one side of the property, the remains of the burnt-out pub rose with its twisted bar furniture warped by the heat of the fire. Yet, on the other side, in the middle of the parking lot, people filled a lighted tent. The sound of conversation, laughter, and music coming from the villagers who had brought their instruments flowed from every side.

My father's calm determination was infectious; our whole village caught the hope and strength to rebuild he exuded. This quiet but powerful resolve was the perfect response to those who had tried to destroy our village's spirit. Ballymagorry saw both the worst of humanity and its best. The collective fortitude was a reminder just how powerful the human spirit is. My father's response to the pub's destruction was, upon reflection, the first time I had seen the power and impact of leadership.

My father did indeed build Ballymagorry Arms again. One year after the bombing, he opened a brand-new pub, bigger and better than the one before. However, there was one major difference: he built our new home at the other end of the parking lot, separate from the pub, just in case. In future years, he bought and sold three more pubs. The pub business played a significant role in my family's collective experience. My four sisters and I grew up working at the pub. We collected empty glasses at first, eventually graduated to serving drinks ourselves, and, finally, managed the pub. We had a love-hate relationship with our family's pub. Our working hours were long and hard, yet the pub was a tremendous source of fun and entertainment for my sisters and me.

Figure 1.3. Family picture, 1974, one year after the bombing. From left to right: my father, Brian, who was a gentle giant of a man; my sisters, Ann, Kate, Mary, and Susan; my beautiful mother, Teresa, whose strength and quiet determination kept us together in the darkest of days; in the front middle, sit I, the youngest of the family and only boy.

The Pub: An Irish Phenomena

The pub is a particularly Irish institution dating back to the very roots of the early Celts. In one of the earliest Celtic settlements 2,570 years ago, archeologists unearthed a central gathering space which had a brewery capable of producing large quantities of beer. They also found charred barley grains, indicating the beer produced had been dark, smoky, and slightly sour.

The Irish are famously credited with saving civilization by Tomas Cahill.[2] He documents St. Patrick's vision of building monastic centers. This vision became a reality and they served as centers of academia, culture, and prosperity. The monks copied all the great classical Greek, Latin, and pagan works. As Europe fell into the Dark Ages, its books were destroyed along with its learning and history. After the Dark Ages, Irish monks established monasteries all over Europe. They brought with them the Irish passion for learning, and with this passion came their books, bookmaking skills, and knowledge. Cahill notes that without these monasteries, "there would have perished in the west not only literacy, but all the habits of mind that encourage thought."[3]

However, the monks also brought the Irish predilection for beer as well as the Christian faith throughout Europe. Perhaps the most famous Irish missionary monk was Columban (540–615 CE). He was born near Dublin in the mid-sixth century and traveled from Ireland to Europe with twelve companions as the first missionary monks. He went on to establish Luxeuil Abbey in France and Bobbio Abbey in Italy. Columban wrote one of the most famous monastic rules governing the monastic way of life. This rule was very strict but did not forbid the consumption of beer. Indeed, there is a penance in the event of spilling beer.

Columban is even reported to have performed a miracle with beer when visiting one of his monasteries. He saw the monks toiling in the field and called them to come in and have a feast. Although there were only two loaves of bread and a little beer, after he offered a prayer, there suddenly was enough for everyone. Of course, we can see the echoes of Jesus's miracle with the loaves and fishes in this legend—except the fish is replaced with beer.

In the seventh century, the law of the land in Ireland was called Brehon Law. This law was ahead of its time in many ways for its compassionate treatment of people. The Irish tradition of hospitality can be seen in part of the law demanding one must feed and care for whomever came to their door with no questions asked. Another part of this law required each local king to have its own *bruigu*, or brewer. The kings were to provide hospitality to everyone in a *bruidean*, or hostel. The law further states that they were to have, "a never-dry cauldron, a dwelling on a public road, and a welcome to every face."[4]

In the tenth century, Saint Bridget was reputed to perform her own beer miracles. One day, while visiting a leper colony, she was distressed to find out that the inhabitants had run out of beer. In an age when water was very often unsafe to drink, beer offered a germ-free alternative. Bridget found a bathtub full of water and turned it into beer for the colony. She also penned one of the most famous poems of the tenth century which begins:

I'd like to give a lake of beer to God.
I'd love the heavenly
Host to be tippling there
For all eternity.

And ends

I'd sit with the men, the women, and God
There by the lake of beer.
We'd be drinking good health forever
And every drop would be a prayer.

With the Norman invasion of Ireland in the twelfth century, the existing tradition of the *bruidean* was augmented with the Norman tradition of the ale house. It was from this new tradition that we began to see the emergence of public houses (from which the word "pub" comes). Indeed, the oldest existing pub in Ireland was established in 1198. The Brazen Head, located in Dublin, is still open for business and offers musical and storytelling evenings along with a great pint of Guinness. During a 1970 renovation, coins dating back to the 1200s were found that, centuries before, had been used as beer tokens for travelers using the premises.

The tradition of the pub is deeply emmeshed in Irish culture. As you can see from this brief history, its function included much more than just the provision of beer and other drink—it was a focal point in the community. The pub was a place of hospitality, a rest stop for those who journeyed, and a place where the great traditions of music and story thrived.

The Pub: A "Third Place"

In *The Great Good Place*, sociologist Ray Oldenburg writes about "third places;"[5] social places apart from home and work, which offer people a space to spend time. He comments that third places are essential to the establishment of strong communities and people's well-being. According to Oldenburg, characteristics of these places include being: a home away from home that engenders feelings of warmth and belonging; full of regulars; fueled by playful and happy conversation; and, finally, a leveling place, where socio-economic status does not count. By these criteria, the pub is very much a "third place."

Where Does Leadership Fit In?

When you first read the title of this book, you might have wondered what leadership has to do with a pub. After all, for many people, the pub is the place they go to forget about work. Yet the pub is one of the oldest types of businesses still in existence today. This history is rich with lessons for leaders and organizations.

If you look at the four characteristics I just mentioned above, it is easy to see how they can be translated into some of the most important organizational and leadership concerns today:

A home away from home. Employees want jobs they actually care about, and they want to know their efforts make a real difference to their teams, managers, and companies.

A place full of regulars. With high turnover and the desire to retain talent, organizations are struggling to provide a sense of belonging in the workplace.

Playful and happy conversation. At the core of any thriving organization is the ability of every employee to feel comfortable enough to contribute and to share and debate ideas.

A leveling place. Organizations are learning that when everyone's background, nationality, and unique qualities are appreciated and workplace diversity thrives, the benefits include new perspectives, a wider talent pool, more innovation, better employee performance, and higher profits.

How do you create such a space in an organization? What must a leader do? Those questions lie at the core of this book. I want to share seven lessons from managing a pub that speak directly to leaders of today.

LESSON #1: You Get To Set The Tone

Leaders can have an impact on the workplace environment by the mood and tone they set.

LESSON #2: You Have The Power To Choose Your Response Even When Triggered

Each day, leaders are triggered emotionally. However, rather than constantly reacting, they can learn to have more choice in their responses.

LESSON #3: You Have The Power To Build Community

The challenge of creating a workplace where employees feel a sense of connection and belonging begins with the leader's example.

LESSON #4: You Are Called To Be A Seanchaí (Storyteller)

Storytelling has the power to engage others and help them to see their work's deeper meaning. The leader must also act as the CSO (Chief Storytelling Officer).

Lesson #5: You Are Called To Be A Bridge, Not A Wall

The leader's example can help change conflict from being destructive to being constructive.

LESSON #6: You Are Called To Hold Space

The leader can help an organization weather whatever challenges it encounters by becoming more resilient. At the core of resilience is the ability to create a space in which optimism, laughter, and difficult emotions can be expressed.

LESSON #7: You Have The Power To Be A Thin Place

Through their very presence, leaders can help employees connect with their hearts, souls, and widen their perspectives.

Before we dig deeper into these seven lessons, let's explore what makes leadership such a difficult task as well as the vital importance of emotional intelligence in managing it. I will also show you how my own life and experience led me to my conclusions.

CHAPTER 2

Not For The Fainthearted

When I tell people that I grew up in a pub, a smile instantly comes to their faces. I get such responses as, "Wow, that must have been so much fun," or "Lucky you, free drinks on the house." They have an idealistic image of what growing up in a pub must have been like. The reality, of course, is very different. The bar business is not an easy life—it requires long hours, an ability to please all types of people, and earns a low margin. To survive and thrive requires deft leadership.

In many ways, leadership can get that reaction. People easily consider all the perks of a job. However, after having worked with leaders as an executive coach, trainer, and speaker, I can honestly say that leadership is not for the faint of heart. It takes courage to step forward and be willing to put yourself on the line. It's been an honor and privilege for me to partner with so many leaders as they struggle in their roles, trying to make the right decisions and creating a workspace they can be proud of.

Why is leadership so difficult? The difficulty lies in the shifting external reality in which all organizations and businesses have to live. This reality, in turn, requires a sophisticated response from leaders, which is grounded in the strength of their emotional intelligence.

The External Reality: A VUCA World

At the end of the Cold War, the US Army War College was charged with mapping out strategy in the uncharted territory we faced as a nation and world. They developed an acronym to conceptualize this territory: VUCA (volatility, uncertainty, complexity, and ambiguity). The reality they were pointing to perfectly explains the difficulty that organizations and their leaders have to confront.

V – Volatility Leaders face increasing speed in the rate of change. Very often, these changes are unpredictable and out of your control. In the first half of 2020, with the spread of the Covid-19 virus, leaders had to react to a situation that was changing by the day—if not the hour. Hard decisions had to be made with limited information. Should we shut down or continue to operate? How do we best protect our employees? How will our supply chain be impacted?

U – Uncertainty We live in a reality where there are no concrete trends or patterns, making it very difficult to predict what will happen. Leaders, however, have to confront uncertainty and prepare for hypothetical situations.

C – Complexity We work in a dynamic environment with many interdependencies. Added to this is the sheer volume of information available to us. It is easy to see how we can become overwhelmed.

A – Ambiguous As a result of the sheer volume of information, people can arrive at different interpretations and hold each of them as equally valid. Fewer and fewer decisions are binary in nature. We have entered the world of gray, where leaders cannot reduce things to a Yes or No. Rather, they live in the tension of decision-making when information points to many options.

The Internal Response

This new world places leaders under enormous pressure and requires a skillset to successfully navigate this reality. At a more basic level, I have noticed with increasing frequency that leaders are emotionally triggered in dealing with these different pressures. This constant triggering has the potential to derail the best of efforts and result in poor decisions. It is imperative that leaders address this new workplace norm.

Expand Your Hardware

Years ago, I was excited to purchase a new graphics program for my computer. It was back when software was sent on a CD-ROM. I installed the program and began to use it. However, it soon became apparent that the software was not operating properly, and everything I did was taking an inordinate amount of time. As I tried to troubleshoot the situation, I soon found out that the issue was not with the software, but with the hardware itself. The software's performance was never going to change unless I upgraded the computer to run the program efficiently.

This example perfectly encapsulates why emotional intelligence is critically important. Organizations in the US spent nearly $90 billion on training in 2018. Leaders are invited to attend every type of skill training from sales to strategic thinking. If we reason that these trainings are like software, it does not matter how wonderful the training is if the capacity of the hardware— that is, the leader—does not expand; they will not run at their full capacity. How do we enlarge the capacity of leaders? By expanding their emotional intelligence.

What Is Emotional Intelligence?

One of the questions I ask during the emotional intelligence training I offer is, "What are some of the qualities of the most memorable leader for whom you've ever worked?" Over the years, I've heard such answers such as:

- They were calm under pressure.
- They were warm.
- They were compassionate.
- They were motivating.
- They were able to coach and mentor me.
- They were able to listen without judgment.

- They were optimistic.
- They had a can-do attitude.

What do all these answers have in common? They are all elements of emotional intelligence. Indeed, about 95 percent of all answers in the list above are in the domain of emotional intelligence.

Emotional intelligence is the ability to recognize, understand, and manage our own emotions and to recognize, understand, and influence the emotions of others. The term was first coined by researchers Peter Salovey and John Mayer and popularized by Daniel Goleman in his 1996 book *Emotional Intelligence.*[6]

Since then, many models of emotional intelligence have been formed, but most of them can be encapsulated into four basic quadrants, as shown in the model below.

◉ AWARENESS	⚙ MANAGEMENT
SELF-AWARENESS	**SELF-MANAGEMENT**
Recognize Emotional Triggers	Choose Balanced Response
Detect Physiological Signals	Self-Motivation
Name Emotions	Display Optimism
SOCIAL AWARENESS	**SOCIAL INTERACTION**
Recognize Emotions in Others	Manage Conflict
Show Empathy	Able to Influence Others
Aware of Group Behavior	Build Teams and Networks

Figure 2.1. The four dimensions of emotional intelligence.

LEADERSHIP LESSONS FROM THE PUB

1. Self-Awareness

"How are you feeling today?" How many times do we ask this question every day? Most of the time, we just want the simple answer, "I'm fine." However, if you want to get to the heart of self-awareness, that's a really important question to ask. How do you feel? Are you able to distinguish one emotion from the other? Are you able to distinguish between anger, sadness, and happiness? What emotion is it? The question isn't only about the emotion, but also that emotion's intensity. So, ask yourself, am I angry, or am I just miffed? Am I angry, or furious, or even explosive? The first aspect of self-awareness is the ability to clearly distinguish one emotion from the other, along with the emotions' varying levels of intensity.

A second element of self-awareness is our ability to be in touch with our body's physiological signs. We live in a world where very often what's required of us is from the neck upward and we ignore the signals our body gives us when we are in the midst of an emotion, before we even become conscious of that emotion. The ability to notice that our body feels tense, or that our heart is beating faster, or that we are now breathing deeper, can give us valuable information that we have, perhaps, been triggered.

That brings us to the final element of self-awareness, our emotional triggers. As I mentioned before, we live in a VUCA world—volatile, uncertain, complex, and ambiguous—

which places a huge strain on us. As a consequence, we are emotionally triggered at work many times each day. If we can understand why we are triggered and how the trigger shows up within us, we have the possibility of responding to the underlying emotion with greater choice.

2. Self-Management

I was in Hawaii a few years ago, and if you've ever been there, you know that some of the beaches are rather hard to find. The only way to get to them is by reading mile markers on the road and trying to find the entrance shortly after that marker. One day, we tried to get to a particular beach and wound up hopelessly lost. We turned down a narrow lane thinking it would lead to the beach. However, we found ourselves pulling up to a small house and separate garage.

We saw a man working in the garage who appeared to be carving a wooden bowl. We asked him about the beach, and as he was explaining how to get there, I became fascinated by the bowl he was carving. I asked him about what he was doing and he began to explain. We ended up spending two or three hours with him while he worked. Next to him, was a huge chest of different instruments.

At certain points, he pulled out one of the instruments and used it to carve a certain way. I asked him how he decided which instrument to use, and he told me that it depended on the thickness of the wood and on what was needed at that moment.

Self-management is just like that. We amass a set of tools that we use in the moment. What do we do when anger is triggered? What do we do when sadness is triggered? How do we respond to an angry boss? How do we respond to a team that's just got no motivation? People who are emotionally intelligent are able to pull out a tool from their self-management kit that helps them manage situations better in the moment.

3. Social Awareness

Social awareness, unlike self-awareness, is awareness that's pointed outward. It's the ability to recognize what's happening with the people around us. Our focus can be on individuals: Their face is the primary and clearest channel of emotion. We can develop the skill to read emotions and detect if people are happy, sad, angry, or disgusted. We can also tell if they are trying to hide these emotions. In addition, we can gather information from their body language, their voice, the flow of the conversation, and the content of the words they use.

Empathy also plays a part in social awareness, because it helps us understand and feel the emotion of another person.

Our focus can also be on groups of people: Social awareness helps us pick up on the mood of a room of people when we walk into a meeting and ascertain if that mood changes. Furthermore, social awareness helps us pick up on relationship dynamics within a group. As you will find out later, my father had an amazing ability to sense what was happening in a group, especially if there might be trouble.

4. Social Interaction

The fourth and final dimension is social interaction, which, simply put, is the ability to manage relationships around you. Having become aware of the communication signals the other person is giving, you are able to adjust in the moment. Social interaction encompasses:

- Building connections with other people

- Productive collaboration with individuals and teams

- Dealing with conflict in a healthy manner

- Developing and mentoring others

- Making decisions; bringing in the thoughts and opinions of others

This inner work lies at the core of leadership development. Indeed, I believe that leaders are developed from the inside out. We cannot skip this part, because it expands the ability to do all the other things required of leaders. Research is replete with evidence of the importance of inner work. Those leaders who have a higher level of emotional intelligence have been shown to be more productive, have lower levels of turnover, higher levels of engagement, and helped create higher profitability.[7]

My Own Journey With Emotional Intelligence

As you know from the opening story in the last chapter, I grew up in the conflict of Northern Ireland. While others born in the same year would later be called Baby Boomers, my generation was called Children of The Troubles. That period had an impact on me in ways that I am still discovering. It's hard to describe the experience of growing up during those years—when I was six, the bombing of our home and business; at nine, seeing shot and wounded policemen sheltering in our home after they had been ambushed; at eleven, narrowly missing a window collapsing on me in school after a huge bomb went off in the adjacent street; and, throughout my childhood, having to be stopped and searched when I went into every store to check for bombs.

One of the impacts of this atmosphere was a constant feeling of fear and anxiety playing in the background and which, at times, would become more pronounced. The need for safety was paramount—in my case, real, physical safety—but this need permeated everything, including the need for emotional safety.

What a blessing, therefore, to have the example of warm and open parents and the dynamics of the family bar, which showed me another reality. In a nation torn apart by hate, anger, and violence, my parents shielded me with love and a belief in the fundamental goodness of people. In a nation broken into warring tribes that could not communicate with each other, I had the example in my home downstairs of a community of friendship, fun and acceptance.

The juxtaposition has continued to play out in my life as I have become more aware of it. I experience an inner tension between seeking safety and shutting down on the one hand, or being open and taking risks, optimistic that things will turn out for the good on the other.

At eighteen, I decided to enter the seminary and become a Catholic priest. Part of that decision was based on a desire to help people. The Catholic Church and my faith had been an important part of my youth. I always marveled at my mother's devotion and faith; it got her though the most harrowing of times. My uncle, after whom I was named, was a priest in Florida. Each summer when he would visit, his joy and down-to-earth approach influenced me considerably. I have to be honest, however, and say that the idea of priesthood also answered my desire for safety. As a priest, I would be protected and cared for. Life would be predictable, and I would not have to map out a path in a world of risk.

I decided to follow my uncle's footsteps and go to Florida to be a priest. I entered All Hallows College seminary, founded in 1842 to send priests with people who fled the Irish famine. The seminary still existed, and everyone who went there continued to serve in locations all over the world. In 1997, I was ordained as a Catholic priest to serve within a five-county region in southeast Florida.

Figure 2.2. Offering my parents a blessing after being ordained a priest.

Seminary, like so many other college professional training programs, does not prepare you for the reality of leading people—in my case, a faith community. I came out of seminary thinking I had all the answers. I shudder to remember how narrow my focus was at that stage of my life.

However, ten years of priesthood taught me that life is anything but black and white. I grew from someone who would offer trite answers into someone who was willing to enter into the struggle of people's lives and accept the mystery and pain of not having adequate answers and the power of silent presence.

The work I was involved in was incredible, from helping refugees from the Guatemalan Civil War, running the local branch of

Catholic Charities, to pastoring one of the largest churches in the area with 5,000 members. The challenges were immense. On a purely emotional level, priesthood is extraordinary. First thing in the morning, you can celebrate the joy of new life at a baptism; later that morning, you can console those grieving at a funeral; in the afternoon, you can celebrate the love of two people at their wedding; and then you can go to your office to counsel someone whose relationship is breaking apart. It was an emotional rollercoaster.

On the outside, I seemed calm, but on the inside, there were all sort of emotions bubbling to the surface, sometimes gently, and other times manifesting in more reactive behavior, such as failing to listen, shutting down conversations, and avoiding conflict. Thankfully, I was blessed to have a very wise and emotionally intelligent spiritual director who journeyed with me during these years.

I had to learn the painful lesson that, for all the degrees and training I had, I was still a novice when it came to understanding my own emotional life. I began to notice and name my own emotions. I saw how emotional triggers that went back to my childhood influenced my present life. When I felt threatened, the desire to protect myself and seek safety led directly to behaviors that shut down conversations and relationships.

As I began to peel back the onion, there was one more layer I had avoided dealing with up to then—my sexuality. Northern Ireland was a very conservative society. While Protestants might have hated Catholics, and vice versa, they both equally hated gay people. While I had known my orientation for many years, I was too fearful to address it, and priesthood provided a life where why I had not married would never be questioned.

As I expanded my emotional self-awareness, I began to understand that if I was to be authentic, I would have to integrate this part of me that I had, in many ways, ignored. That act of self-integration finally led me to leave the priesthood. I had come to the conclusion that I wanted to be in a loving relationship, and I was not prepared to live a celibate life anymore. It was one of the most difficult decisions I have ever made, yet it was the correct one for me.

After leaving the priesthood, I went on to lead a social service agency for six years. At the core of this experience was the understanding that, no matter how skilled I was at doing various tasks, my lack of emotional intelligence got in the way at various times. My desire to avoid conflict and confrontation because of a deep-seated need to be safe led to some very poor decisions. However, I could also see real growth in the ways I managed conflicting personalities and exercised the power I had to create a positive work environment.

During this time, I was also finishing up with my doctorate in management. I was researching how CEOs dealt with issues of accountability and transparency, especially in times of great crisis. My research took me deeper into the world of emotional intelligence and how it impacted leadership. From that vantage point, I could see a deeper mission for myself: to actively help leaders expand their emotional intelligence in order to have more impact.

In 2013, I made another huge decision. I quit my job and moved to Washington DC. I wanted to start my own company which would let me focus my new mission. The move also would allow me to be with my partner—now husband—who lived in that city.

As I have continued this work, I have realized that the leadership journey is not a straight path forward. My work takes me into the offices of many leaders. Expanding our emotional intelligence is not easy. There is no quick fix. One day, we may think we have it all together, only to be surprised the next day at how triggered we have become. I constantly revisit the example of my parents and the experience of growing up in the pub. The lessons I learned there made me a better leader, and I have found the lessons have also resonated with the leaders I've worked with. I have refined the lessons down to the most important ones. Let's journey back to Northern Ireland and jump into the first.

CHAPTER 3

Mind The Craíc!

LESSON #1: *You Get To Set The Tone*

I f an Irish pub is going to be successful, there needs to be plenty of craíc. Indeed, if the craíc is not plentiful and of the finest quality, a pub just will not survive.

When I talk about craíc in a presentation, I usually get a few who look at me horrified as if I am referring to a den of iniquity full of drugs. There is no difference in the pronunciation between the words crack and craíc, but there is a world of a difference in the words' meaning.

Craíc is the Irish word for "fun atmosphere" and describes the ambience and enjoyment you have in the pub. A morning conversation at the coffee shop might sound like:

"Shelia, where did you go last night?"

"Ah, Shelia, sure, I went to Doyle's Pub."

"How was the craíc?"

"Sure, it was brilliant."

Now the craíc is not the same in every pub. A mysterious ingredient, craíc has the power to make the difference between a dull evening and one with intense conversation and fun. Without good craíc, a pub will be in trouble. In 2014, Dave Infante wrote an article in Thrillist about the dramatic growth in the popularity of Irish pubs.[8] Companies will ship you everything you need, from furniture to memorabilia, to open an Irish pub in your local area. You can even choose your style of pub. They come in three main varieties:

1. The Country Cottage Pub

This design attempts to replicate a traditional style of an Irish country cottage. Wooden beams and stone floors reflect the reality that the first pubs were homes which had a tradition of being so welcoming that they simply became accepted as the local pub. The owner simply put their last name over the door to attract customers.

Figure 3.1. The Rusty Mackerel, Carrick, Co. Donegal, Ireland.

2. The Shop Pub

This style reflects the tradition of a grocery or hardware story doubling up as a pub. This pub has shelves filled with soap, sugar, and hardware to evoke the spirit of a one-stop shop for all the village's needs.

Figure 3.2. Leonard's Pub in Lahardaun, Co. Mayo, Ireland. One of the few pubs left that has a shop built into the pub.

3. The Brewery Pub

This style dates back to the eighteenth-century tradition of a brewery with cobblestone floors and lots of brewing memorabilia reminiscent of the Guinness brewery at St James' Gate in Dublin.

Figure 3.3. The Duke of York Pub in Belfast, Northern Ireland.

After you have chosen your pub style, the company will work with you to find the best location. Two months later, they ship the inside of the pub for you to set up. It all sounds so simple, but alas—not so. The experience of running a pub is something different from simply having the right decor. Many of the new pubs failed in the first six months. At issue, of course, is our friend the craíc. You can have all the furniture and authentic memorabilia you want, but what's missing is the friendly warmth, humor, and advice of a true Irish bartender. Authenticity does not come from the furniture; it is something the owner instills in the pub environment. The owner's ability to set the tone permits the craíc to thrive.

My father naturally exuded authenticity. There was a genuineness about him that radiated outward to others. He was keenly aware that how he showed up each day was of supreme importance. He once told me, "Whatever mood you are in will be reflected back to you by the customers within an hour." How right he was.

I wonder if my father learned this from the farm. You see, as well as getting into the pub business, my father also ran a farm that mainly consisted of cattle grazing the fields. He was tending to both places. I liked nothing better than to spend hours watching the cows. When I was around seven, my father installed an electric fence on one section of the farm to keep the cows from wandering into the next property. Now, for an seven-year-old this fence was a thing of wonder. I remember asking my father what would happen if I touched the fence.

"Son, if you touch that fence your hand is going to burn and drop off," he warned me in his thick Northern Irish accent. That warning was enough to scare the bejesus out of me. However, it did not last long, as there is nothing quite as strong as the curiosity of a child. I can remember sitting at the fence and touching it with a stick to see if there would be sparks. I was disappointed to see there were none. Still not wanting to touch it myself, I was hoping for the next best thing, which was that one of the cows would accidentally touch it. Well, one day I got my wish. One of the cows got a little too close and touched the fence. She let out a loud noise and ran back into the center of the field. I was interested to see that all the other cows also ran to the same place and surrounded her. Now, just one cow had hit the fence, but her fear had spread like lightening to every other cow in the field.

We like to think that as human beings we are very sophisticated, and indeed we are; however, we are closer to those cows than we would like to think. Just like those cows, we can catch the emotions of other people very rapidly. In the pub, my father always knew he had the responsibility to set to the tone and make sure the craíc was as good as it could be. The demands facing most leaders, like the demands of owning a bar and being the boss, may seem glamorous, but in truth, a leader's life is not easy. For my father, there certainly were perks being the boss, but like most leaders, he had long hours of hard work that were unknown to others.

In fact, the first time I can remember my parents and four sisters vacationing together was when I was thirty, and they came to visit me in Florida for my ordination to the priesthood. They had just sold the pub and were free to come. Previously, the whole time my father owned the pub, one member of the family always had to stay home and tend the customers. Growing up, there were many times that I knew my father was tired, and perhaps the last thing he wanted was to serve customers. However, when he entered the pub, he would crack a smile so big that it spread from ear to ear. His energy was restored as he greeted everyone; his positivity and friendliness radiated and filled the pub. I remember watching him work his way to each customer. He would have a chat or a laugh with each one. He was the catalyst for the great craíc.

You Spread Your Emotions

I share this message when I coach leaders from all types of organizations: Leaders have the power to set the tone. Setting the tone is a power they often forget that they have. This message is not just my opinion; it also backed by solid scientific research. We now understand that our emotions are contagious. We can literally "catch" the emotions of others. This infectiousness was a very deliberate design feature of human beings, helping us to survive.

When it comes to our emotions and motivation, one of the most important areas of the brain is called the limbic center. The limbic center functions in an open loop manner, managing emotions by our external connection with other people. Why was this skill important for our survival? Imagine walking past a person who is doubled over in pain. What is the first reaction you might have? We instinctually want to intervene and offer any help we can. If we had a closed system, we would be able to pass this poor person and remain unaffected by their pain. Just like the cows, we are able to sense the fear and anxiety of others and be alerted to potential danger.

Of course, we are not aware that this process is occurring. Some fascinating research from Aalto University in Finland showed that when we are in conversation with another person and feel strong emotions, the brain activities of each person begin to sync with the other. This syncing process aids our ability to understand each other.[9] In addition, research from the University of Colorado, Boulder, also points to the power of touch. In that experiment, scientists found that when an empathetic partner holds the hand of a woman in pain, their heart and respiratory rates sync, and her pain begins to dissipate.[10] This physical process of empathy holds true in all aspects of life, from the office to the home. We call this phenomenon "emotional contagion." Although the word contagion might evoke some negative imaginary, it holds true for all emotions, be they anger, sadness, fear, happiness, or joy.

The impact of emotional contagion becomes even more apparent when we consider the role of a leader. When a leader is in the room, they are carefully watched. I remember coaching one leader who said one of the things she had to get used to in her role was that in meetings, people would make comments and then look at her to get an indication if she was supportive or not. What she said in meetings was often quoted and misquoted by others after the meeting.

This leader's comments are totally in line with the researchers' findings, which include:

- A correlation between a leader's display of happiness and displeasure and employee performance.[11]

- A leader's negative emotion directly impacts levels of trust and team member relationships.[12]

- Leaders who showed more positive emotions during their interactions caused employees to experience more positive emotions. The reverse was also found to be true; employees reported less job satisfaction and increased stress when they experienced negative emotions from their supervisors.[13]

It is interesting to note this impact is also felt by employees who might not have a leadership title, but are looked up to by other employees.

Daniel Goleman, the person who first popularized the term emotional intelligence, uses the image of a big soup pot to explain the phenomenon of emotional contagion at work.[14] Every day, every person in the organization adds flavoring to the soup, which everyone consumes. However, it the flavor of the leader that is the strongest and has the greatest impact on the taste of the soup. Every day in the workplace, we are adding our emotions and moods. It's critical for leaders to ask the simple yet profound question, "What seasoning am I adding to the workplace today?" The answer to this question will have an impact on what happens that day. The leader's seasoning has the power to increase or decrease employee satisfaction and level of performance. Over a longer period, this seasoning has an impact on employee retention and turnover.

I remember seeing this phenomenon in my first job out of college. I was always fascinated by the idea of being in the Foreign Service, and my childhood dream job was to become an ambassador. I decided to get a summer intern job and build up my resumé in one of the local government offices close to the university. Now, truth be told, I was nothing more than someone who ran errands, delivered the mail, and made tea when called upon. My friend, Gerard, already worked there, and wanting to make a good impression, I asked him if he had any tips. He replied that I needed to befriend Sally, the receptionist for the whole imposing Victorian building. She knew everything that was happening. So, for the next few weeks I did everything I could to befriend her. I complemented her on her clothes and hair and I made sure her tea was with two sugars the way she liked it. Luckily for me, I think she felt sorry for this awkward twenty-two-year-old guy with the Irish accent.

One morning, as I was walking past Sally on my way into the building, she gave me a thumbs up sign. I had no idea what she was referring to, so I gave her a thumbs up back. At lunchtime, I ran into Gerard and asked him about this mysterious sign. He replied that I had succeeded in getting my "in" with Sally as the thumbs up was part of her secret messaging system. A thumbs up meant that the boss had arrived in a good mood, while a thumbs down meant that he had arrived in a bad mood. I would later learn that the latter event was known, internally, as the boss having an "unmedicated" day. However, the behaviors I noticed with those two signals were extraordinary. When I delivered the mail on thumbs up days, the doors of the corridor were open; I could hear people in conversation and the sounds of laughter. On thumbs down days, the opposite was true.

There was silence in the corridors. Doors were closed and you could feel the tension in the air. After lunch, there were quite a few who did not return and instead ducked out for the rest of the day.

Here's the moral of the story: Leaders have the power to create a thumbs up or thumbs down day. In 2020, we also saw how the power of a virus, COVID-19, invisible to the eye, could impact our behavior. So, it is with emotions as well—they are invisible, but as soon as we walk through the door, we can catch other people's emotions. Because of their unique position, leaders need to be very aware of the emotions they sow each day.

The importance of emotional contagion is even more apparent in the way we deal with our emotional triggers. We'll turn to this topic in our next chapter.

Chapter Activities

At the end of each of the seven lessons you will find two sections to help you reflect and take action on content of the chapter.

1. Lesson Inventory

You will be invited to rate yourself along a continuum to help you assess what areas are strengths and what areas might need development.

I am aware of my emotional state before I enter any meeting	Almost Never True	Almost Always True

2. Lesson Toolbox

The toolbox will list a number of exercises and practices related to the questions that were just answered. They provide practical tools and activities to strengthen and develop the areas mentioned in the previous chapter. These tools and activities can be found in a mini course which I have especially developed for this book.

Please visit the following link to access the course:
www.leadershiplessonsfromthepub.com/toolbox

▌Lesson 1 Inventory

Reflect on the statement and how you typically "show up" at work. Think of examples in your experience. Place an "X" along the continuum that best reflects you.

I am aware of my emotional state before I enter any meeting.	Almost Never True	Almost Always True
I am aware when my mood changes because of the presence or words of another person.	Almost Never True	Almost Always True
I find it difficult to read the emotional cues of others?	Almost Never True	Almost Always True
I am able to alter my frame of mind or mood.	Almost Never True	Almost Always True

▌Lesson 1 Toolbox

Reflect on the statement and how you typically "show up" at work. Think of examples in your experience. Place an "X" along the continuum that best reflects you.

Please visit **www.leadershiplessonsfromthepub.com/toolbox**

1. 7-Second Reset.
2. Body Scan.
3. Mindfully Entering Work And Home.
4. What Is Self-Awareness And Why It Is Important?

CHAPTER 4

I'm Triggered, Now What?

LESSON #2: *You Have The Power To Choose Your Response Even When You Are Triggered*

Have you ever said Yes to something and only a few hours later regretted it? One of those happened to me on July 23, 2002. I had received a phone call from Henry, the chair of the board of directors for a local affiliate of a national organization.

"Irvine, I am calling to let you know that the board of directors just met and unanimously agreed to offer you the position of CEO." As someone who was looking for the opportunity to lead their first organization, these were magical words.

Without a moment of hesitation, I said, "Henry, I am honored by your confidence in me and I look forward to working with you and the rest of the board." Later that afternoon, as

I thought about the organization and the 450 employees for whom I would responsible, my excitement turned into a little bit of anxiety.

The first day at my new position proved even more interesting. I am not sure if this has ever happened to you, but the organization that had been described in glowing terms during the interview process was nothing of the sort. Personnel issues that had been swept under the carpet now began to rear their ugly heads and were knocking at my door. The majority of the staff were on edge because of persistent rumors leading them to believe severe budget cuts were imminent. The financials were a lot worse than had been indicated, and income had come up short three years in a row. What's more, there was the pervasive thought that these problems would somehow magically work themselves out, except no one had given me a magic wand.

As I prepared for the first board meeting, I grew increasingly uneasy. The board, who had "unanimously" approved my hiring, were anything but united; they were deeply divided with five on one side and six on another.

I had just implemented some changes in the organization and there was considerable pushback. What's more, the grumbling had made its way to the boardroom and fallen on receptive ears. At last, the board found something they could all agree upon, namely, their disappointment and hostility toward me. I felt like a student in the headmaster's office. What was more, I was totally triggered by the situation and froze like a defenseless animal as the vultures picked me apart. I remember leaving the meeting, going to the bathroom, and actually throwing up. When I got to the office of the COO, she took one look at me and said, "Wow, that bad."

Luckily for me, the following week I had to go to Ireland for a wedding, and there is nothing like an Irish wedding to drown your sorrows. The day after the wedding, my father and I decided to go to a pub for a drink and a chat. As we settled in with our drinks, I started to tell him my tale of woe. He listened and smiled. He had this amazing ability to just be present, as if you were the only person in the world at the moment. I remember him saying to me, "Irvine, it sounds like they have you in a right old state. Remember, you get to choose your response." Of course, he was correct. I had been triggered in that board meeting and I was reacting from a place of feeling threatened. I had shut down rather than notice what was happening to me and choosing a different response.

My father went on to chat about how in the pub, just like at home, people know how to press each other's buttons and get them going. His customer's reactions were all over the place. However, after a while, he noticed what triggered a customer was different for each one, as was their reaction to it. Johnny, for example, would fall silent and go into himself while a sadness took over his face. Micky would get defensive and began to argue back. Mary would laugh it off, but my father could see she was hurt.

Sometimes, people would be so triggered that the words that got them going turned out to be fighting words. My father was always on the lookout for the telltale signs that a fight might be coming. He used to say, "Be careful when the monkey is beating his breast." He was referring to the fact that as people prepared to fight, they puffed out their chests and jutted out their chins. As soon as he saw these signs, he knew what was coming next and jumped in to intervene. As a side note, one of the most amazing sights I have ever seen was my father lifting a man who was about to fight by the back of the neck and taking him outside to cool off.

When I returned to my new job after that trip to Ireland, I began the long journey of exploring what had triggered me and how I had a tendency to shut down in conflict. Of course, the challenges of the organization did not disappear, but I grew less defensive and worked with the board through some very difficult decisions.

Learn How To Manage Your Triggerprint

As human beings, we are wonderfully made. One function overrides all others—survival. We are constantly looking around our environment to see if there are any threats. It's like we have an internal radar constantly scanning the environment. All of this happens outside of our awareness. When something is determined to be a threat, a highly sophisticated and coordinated program is activated; it's primary focus is to keep us safe. It happens so quickly that the program is activated before we are even aware of an immediate threat. What are some of the steps of that program?

1. The brain shortcuts information being passed through the neocortex, which is the home of conscious thought and reason and goes to the amygdala, which modulates our response in times of threat. This response is not surprising, as when we see potential danger on the horizon, it is less important to think about what is happening than it is to react in the moment.

2. Our heart begins to beat harder and faster so it can send oxygen and adrenalin to supply energy to our arms and legs as we prepare to fight or flee.

3. Our breathing rate increases so we can have more oxygen in our blood system.

4. Adrenaline is sent to the eyes and our pupils become dilated so we can see better. Our peripheral vision is also heightened.

5. Our digestive system is radically reduced, because eating is not critical to answering this threat. That is why, just as in my situation with the board meeting, some people can get physically sick when they feel threatened.

6. The mouth reduces its amount of saliva production, leading to dry mouth.

7. With your muscles full of oxygen and primed to act, they can also begin to shake.

If you are reading this book, give thanks for this amazing program because it worked, and you survived. When our ancestors woke up and came out of the cave for the day and saw a woolly tooth mammoth coming near, they did not think to themselves, "Oh look, a large animal is looking at me and seems to be angry. I wonder if I should I run?" No, their reactions were instantaneous. However, today, that program can also get in the way of logic. The brain does not do a great job of differentiating between dangers that are life-threatening and emotional triggers that are not life-threatening. The problem is, our body reacts the same way.

We all have a unique fingerprint, but we also have a unique triggerprint; a word I created to explain the uniqueness in each of our emotional triggers. This is hardly surprising considering how our life experiences are so different. As leaders, it's essential that each of us knows what our own triggerprint is because it will dramatically impact our performance in that moment. As an executive leadership coach, I have heard many different triggers from clients:

- The words budget cuts in any organization

- As the workplace becomes more complex, being left out of the loop

- Receiving a negative or a sarcastic remark at a meeting

- Being talked over at a meeting

- A supervisor's bad mood

- One client referred to urgency mismatch: Your request to an employee, which you considered urgent, was dealt with as something unimportant

- Employees who do not deliver on assigned tasks

- The announcement of big changes

- Being rude to another employee in front of everyone else

- Having to deal with an angry customer

The list could go on and on because everyone's triggerprint is different. I always suggest to leaders I am working with to reflect on their triggers and to come up with their own list.

Why is it important to know our unique triggerprint? Because of its impact on our performance. Remember that when we feel under threat and are triggered, our brain shortcuts information going to the neocortex. This shortcutting process influences our ability to learn and to be curious. With the lack of curiosity comes a tendency to see everything in binary terms. The answer is either "This" or "That." Leaders I have coached also mention their tendency to make decisions quickly in order to drop the tension they feel. Some will become defensive and more argumentative, while others will shut down—just as I did at the board meeting—and go silent. All of these behaviors prevent leaders from functioning at their best, especially in critical moments for their organizations.

The good news is that there are a number of different practices we can implement to help us in the moment we are triggered. These practices aim to introduce choice into our reactions, so that we can pause instead of immediately going into a reactive response. Let's explore two practices leaders I've worked with have found most usfeul.

Practice #1: 7-Second Reset

This is a quick way of calming ourselves and making adjustments in the moment. It can be done anywhere, even in the middle of a meeting.

Step 1: Take one second to place your feet on your ground. Feel the physicality of your foot touching the ground. This simple act grounds you in the present moment and begins to detach you from the emotional response you are in.

Step 2: Take three seconds to inhale deeply. Become aware of any tension in your body and of your posture. Are you signaling closed body language which might indicate you have shut down, or are you noticing tension in your hands and more aggressive body language? Imagine sending your breath to any place in your body where you are tense.

Step 3: Take three seconds to breath out slowly. As you breathe out, relax your jaw, shoulders, and chest. Feel your feet on the floor once again. Make any adjustments to your posture to make it more open or less aggressive.

Of course, there is nothing new in this practice, but the real difficulty is remembering to do it in the moment. I created a free daily reminder to practice the seven-second reset, and it includes daily reflection questions for ninety days— the time required to develop a new habit. You can find it at www.7secondreset.com.

Practice #2: Visualize A Different Response To A Trigger

Visualization has been proven to be a very powerful way of developing new skills faster. When we visualize an action, the same region of the brain is stimulated as if we were actually performing the action. Recently, I had a group of surgeons in my training program, and many spoke about how they use the power of visualization before operations in order to go through the procedure, step-by-step, that they are about to perform.

Step 1: Make yourself comfortable and relax. Take a minute to focus on your breathing.

Step 2: Bring to mind the trigger you want to explore. Close your eyes if it is comfortable, and visualize the trigger and your present response when it occurs.

Step 3: Now visualize the same trigger, but this time, replace the old automatic response with the new behavior that you would like to see yourself doing. Try and bring as much detail to this visualization as possible. Involve as many of your senses as you can: sight, sound, touch, smell, and taste. Repeat this visualization often, and certainly before a situation that potentially gives rise to the trigger.

We live in a time when we and the organizations we lead are becoming more complex, and the pace of change is intensifying. As we struggle to deal with this "new normal," we inhabit an environment that has the potential to trigger us multiple times a day. Those who have taken the time to explore their own triggers and response patterns are at a distinct advantage and have the potential to lead with greater calm and, ultimately, make better decisions.

This willingness to explore one's triggers is also key in the ability to build community, especially in times of organizational stress, which is the subject of the next chapter.

Lesson 2 Inventory

Reflect on the statement and how you typically "show up" at work. Think of examples in your experience. Place an "X" along the continuum that best reflects you.

Statement	Almost Never True		Almost Always True
I am aware of those situations that trigger me negatively.			
In stressful situations I can fly off the handle at other people.			
I can recognize my emotions as I experience them?			
I know how to calm myself down when I feel anxious or upset?			

Lesson 2 Toolbox

Please visit www.leadershiplessonsfromthepub.com/toolbox

1. Finding Your Unique Triggerprint.
2. Exercise.
3. Getting On The Balcony.
4. 5 Steps For Managing Your Emotional Triggers.

CHAPTER 5

Here Comes Everybody

LESSON #3: *You Have The Power To Build Community*

When I left high school, I went to the seminary to become a priest. The seminary was full of some great characters. One that stands out was Father Kilty, who seemed to be older than God. He was an incredibly intimidating figure who did not suffer fools. During our first class with him, he got frustrated at our lack of knowledge. He went to the back of the classroom and looked out the window to a pond outside. He remarked loudly, "I might as well be teaching the ducks in the pond."

He also taught us the class about confession. In the introductory class he asked us, "Where are the three most popular places for confession?" We scratched our heads slightly confused by the question. Eventually, I raised my hand and said very proudly,

"An airplane that is about to crash land." Father Kilty took glee in saying, "No." "A ship that is sinking," said Tom. Again, the answer was "No."

Finally, delighted that he had stumped us, he gave us the answer. "Number three is a taxicab, number two is the hair salon, and number one is the pub." He was not speaking about the formal sacrament of confession celebrated mostly in a church. Rather, he was speaking of where people felt comfortable to talk about the good and bad; places people talked about their struggles to someone who would listen and acknowledge them. As I thought about growing up in the pub, I instantly knew that he was 100 percent correct.

Over the past ten years, a set of alarming statistics has emerged concerning workplace engagement. A 2016 Gallup survey found that only 33 percent of employees are engaged; 51 percent are not engaged and have not been for some time. Furthermore, 85 percent of employees are either actively looking for or are open to new employment options. One study of this phenomenon put the potential cost of disengagement between $450 and $500 billion. That means every disengaged employee can cost a company $3,400 per year for every $10,000 of salary.

Those are staggering figures and a huge challenge for leaders. The pub, however, has many insights on engagement and the power of building community where customers feel they belong and are fiercely loyal through thick and thin. Father Kilty's insight into confession is at the core of this phenomenon.

The pub is more than a place to go and have a drink. It is much more than that. Indeed, my father used to say, "I am not in the business of selling drink, rather I am offering a home where everyone is welcome." The pub is a community. It is a place to meet neighbors and friends. It is a place where people felt accepted and included, warts and all. The pub is a safe space. It's only possible to be vulnerable if you feel that you are on friendly ground. It is their local, a place where they belong. The pub is a place where people can be real and where the messiness of life is accepted and celebrated. In many ways, it is a living version of Facebook, where people update others on what is happening in their lives.

The pub is also a place where strangers are welcomed and brought into the circle. When someone new walks into a pub, it is not long before someone is chatting with them and asking them their name and where they are from. While this inquisitiveness might make some uncomfortable, it comes from a place of genuine curiosity and a desire to bring the stranger into the fold.

My father took this practice to another level. Northern Ireland was a deeply divided society and pubs were part of that division. There were Catholic pubs and Protestant pubs. My father, however, welcomed everyone into our pub. He did not mind who came through the door, "So long as they kept the peace." He created a space where both parts of the community were able to coexist.

It is interesting that one of the terms and images commonly used for a publican (the owner of the pub) in Ireland was a priest. The similarity comes from the fact that the two people's duties were often very similar. The owner was seen as taking care of their flock. The pub was the center of some of the most important celebrations—births, christenings, first holy communions, weddings, wakes, and funerals. I remember my father would help people who could not pay for these ceremonial occasions; he put the debt on the slate to be paid over many months or just forgotten about.

As an aside, it was also not uncommon for publicans to double as undertakers. The cold room in the pub became a natural location to place bodies as they were prepared for burial. This was only one of the many services that the local publican provided for the community. Pubs often had groceries, hardware, and other provisions. I remember as a child visiting a friend whose father owned a pub in Newry and playing in the back yard between the beer kegs and the empty caskets. Thankfully, my father never became an undertaker. I am not quite sure how the rest of the family might have felt, knowing the dead were resting in the basement.

I began to see the truth in this sense of community when I became a priest. My role as leader, celebrant, confessor, teacher, and mentor was closer to the work my father did than I imagined.

The publican was also sought out in times of crisis. In many ways, he was often more approachable than the local priest.

I can remember customers pouring their hearts out to my father. It was easy for them, as my father was a familiar figure who was easy to chat with and who never made harsh judgments. Thomas Burke aptly described the qualities that make a great publican: "It is a job that calls for patience, tact, understanding, wise interests, and a love of mankind."[15] He continued, "A publican must know something of everything and be something of a psychologist."

What my father had managed to do—indeed what all good publicans do—was create a space where people felt safe to be vulnerable and to open up. A space where people did not fear that the information they shared would be used against them. A space, not of judgment, but of curiosity and the ability to look with honesty at the human condition. This space is created with a combination of an intense ability to listen, and an empathy that helps people understand and feel they are not alone with their worries and concerns. A space where someone else really cares.

If You Build It, They Will Stay

One of the core needs of any human being is the need to belong; it's built into our DNA. The sense of belonging also includes the workplace, which, considering that we spend approximately one third of our lives at work, is not surprising. Research shows, however, that we are not doing of good job of this. A study conducted by Cigna reported that 39 percent of those interviewed felt ignored in the workplace and 25 percent felt lonely.[16] Imagine going to work each day and day feeling ignored and lonely? It's obvious we have a crisis with engagement. The answer to this lack of engagement is the creation of a sense of belonging. Research from the Center for Talent Innovation found that employees who felt a sense of belonging at work were 3.5 times more likely to be productive, motivated, and engaged.[17] How does a leader build a sense of belonging?

In 2016, Google set about to find the answer to the question, "What makes a team effective?" They choose 188 teams to examine in depth. The researchers examined a host of different variables like team composition (demographics, personality traits, and sales skills) and the team's dynamics. They conducted in-depth interviews as well as countless assessments. Their findings surprised everyone: The makeup of the team in terms of age, experience, location, and gender were not as important as how well the team worked together. The most important variables included dependability, clarity, meaning, and impact. However, one variable was found to be the most important—a sense of psychological safety.

Psychological safety at work refers to the belief that if I partake in learning behaviors such as asking for help, admitting that I made a mistake, asking for feedback, risking something new, or raising a dissenting opinion, I will not be exposed to threats to myself or my identity. My willingness to take a chance will not have an impact on my career or employment. I will not be labelled as ignorant, incompetent, negative, or disruptive. Further research, appearing in the Journal of Management and Organization (2014),[18] backed these initial findings and showed a workplace absent of those threats has higher retention and productivity rates, as well as better decision-making.

How, then, can a leader instill a sense of psychological safety in the workplace? I think it is clear that long before the Google study, pubs and pub culture had cracked the nut on engagement and psychological safety. Here are three elements that can guide the leader and give insight into increasing engagement:

1. The Importance Of Empathy

The High-Resolution Leadership Report by DDI (2020) assessed the behaviors of 15,000 leaders in 300 different companies in eighteen countries over fifteen years and found one surprising behavior that was essential for business success: empathy.[19] Leaders with higher levels of empathetic skills showed 40 percent higher ratings in overall performance, planning, and decision-making. The companies they work for showed higher levels of engagement.

Why is empathy so important? Empathy comes from the Greek, *em* + *pathos*, which literally means "in feeling". It's easy to see here the movement is toward another person, into their feelings. Empathy is the ability to identify and understand another's situation, feelings, and motives. It's our capacity to recognize the concerns other people have. It means putting yourself in another person's shoes or seeing things through someone else's eyes.

At the core of empathy is connection. Empathy requires the ability to be with someone without judgment and take in their perspective. It's not hard, therefore, to see how essential it is in leadership, and as a prerequisite for a leader who wishes to develop and grow psychological safety in the organization. While empathy is critical, it is also a skill many leaders feel they lacked. A University of Michigan study found that only 40 percent of leaders felt they had adequate levels of empathy.[20]

The good news is that empathy, just like other elements of emotional intelligence, can be increased. Let me point to two interesting ways you might want to consider:

A. Read Fiction

As a busy leader, you might not consider you have the time or luxury to read fiction. However, by doing that very thing you are also increasing your level of empathy. Research form Erasmus University in the Netherlands, which has been replicated in other studies, found there is a direct correlation between those that spent time reading fiction (in this case books by Arthur Conan Doyle) and a significant increase in empathy.[21]

It's not hard to see the reason for this correlation—readers are transported to another world when they read and are exposed to all types of experiences and emotions. Recently, I reread *Hotel on the Corner of Bitter and Sweet* by Jamie Ford. It was a gripping love story which spanned many decades. In reading that book, I entered into different emotional experiences of love, joy, abandonment, betrayal, fear, terror, guilt, and blame. The next time you don't think you have time for a great novel, think again and consider it part of developing your emotional intelligence.

B. Widen Your Circle Of Acquaintances

Who is in your circle of friends? How diverse is your circle? Psychology has long known there is such a thing as in-group bias which is the tendency for people to favor those who are part of their group and who display the group's characteristics. This tendency becomes even more pronounced when there is any conflict between groups. However, research also shows that this in-group bias is malleable. A study from the University of Queensland in Australia found that exposure to people who are different from us racially increases the level of empathy we feel toward them when they are in pain.[22] If you want to increase your level of empathy, widen your circle and get friendly with a wide range of people who are not normally part of your group.

2. Sharpen Your Listening Skills

We mentioned earlier in this chapter the importance of employees feeling like they belonged. We also pointed to a high incidence among employees of feeling ignored. Therefore, listening is an essential leadership skill. We live in such a fast-paced world where every second counts that we forget about the power of listening and the impact it has on another person to truly feel they have been acknowledged and heard. It was one of the great qualities both my parents possessed; they could make you feel like you were the only person in the room.

I remember many people came to visit my mother. When she opened the door, she would take one look at their faces and know something was weighing them down. She would invite them in to the kitchen, sit them down, and put on the tea. She did very little talking but lots of listening. When the person left, their burden had lightened. My mother used to say, "Tea can solve all the problems in the world." I now understand she was not referring to actual tea drinking, but rather the ritual of taking time to listen deeply to another person. It has incredible power.

To develop your listening skills, it's important to first explore some of the barriers you have that prevents you from fully listening. There are a number of common ones we all experience:

Rehearsing—Thinking about what you are going to say next and missing what is begin said now.

Daydreaming—Thinking about other things that are coming up later in the day and not being present to the things being said now.

Comparing—Taking what the other person is saying and then comparing it with your own experience.

Mind-reading—Assuming you know what the other person is thinking and feeling without exploring their experience with other questions.

There are also a number of behaviors leaders can embrace to help expand their listening skills:

Don't interrupt—Nothing gives the signal I am not listening more than interrupting a person mid-flow. Give them a chance to finish before responding.

Be curious—It's easy to make judgments about what people are saying. However, if you can suspend judgment and be curious, you may be amazed at things you hear that you might otherwise have missed.

Ask questions—Great leaders ask great questions. Take some time to ask a few questions, so you have a fuller picture of what the person is saying.

Watch your body language—It communicates a message. Does your body language convey that you are listening? Do you have an open stance? Are you making adequate eye contact? Have you slightly moved forward to show you are engaged?

Put your phone away—I find nothing is more distracting than mobile phones. Having a phone in front of you causes too much temptation to glance at it from time to time. It's hard not to be distracted when you see it light up with a new message.

Acknowledge emotions—It's vital to show people that you understand where they are coming from by naming some of the emotions they might be feeling; you can acknowledge how someone is feeling without having to agree with them.

3. Lead By Example

We explored the importance of setting the tone and how a leader's emotions are contagious throughout the whole organization in Chapter 3. In trying to establish a psychologically safe workplace, it's vital for each leader to model the behavior they want to see.

Acknowledge your mistakes—Every organization has a culture around mistakes. If you want to create an organization that rewards creativity, then how you deal with mistakes will be critical. Are you willing to acknowledge your mistakes? If mistakes are made, do you tend to blame others, or do you count the mistakes as important learning steps?

Be approachable—How approachable are you? How open are you to opinions that might differ from yours? How open are you to seeing that others are confident enough to ask questions? Are you careful to listen to everybody's voice? Who might be missing at the table?

Encourage feedback—It's vital that feedback is seen not as criticism but as important data to help performance and decision-making. As a leader, do you seek out feedback? What is the tone of the feedback you give?

The community we build is critical on so many levels. Leaders must help create a space where employees feel they belong and are heard. One building block of community is the story. Let's explore the story's incredible power in the next chapter.

Lesson 3 Inventory

Reflect on the statement and how you typically "show up" at work. Think of examples in your experience. Place an "X" along the continuum that best reflects you.

I find it easy to build rapport with others?	Almost Never True	Almost Always True

I easily see things from another person's point of view?	Almost Never True	Almost Always True

I know which barriers get in the way of my listening.	Almost Never True	Almost Always True

I listen to others without feeling the need to interrupt.	Almost Never True	Almost Always True

Lesson 3 Toolbox

Please visit www.leadershiplessonsfromthepub.com/toolbox

1. Character Emotions.
2. Who's In My Circle?
3. Find My Listening Blocks.
4. How To Be A Better Listener.

CHAPTER 6

Fado Fado
(Once Upon A Time)

LESSON #4: *You Are Called To Be A Seanchaí*
(Storyteller)

I always loved visiting my Auntie Betty. There was something special about the twinkle in her eye, her laugh was infectious, and she loved a great story. I remember a trip a few years ago; it was the first trip to Ireland for my husband, Fred. We decided to visit Auntie Betty first thing after our overnight flight to Dublin. A three-hour drive later, we arrived at her house in Omagh at 10 a.m.

Auntie Betty was so excited to meet Fred. We were welcomed with big hugs and brought into the front room. Five minutes later, she arrived with a bottle of whiskey and a few bottles of Budweiser. "Sure, you'll have a wee drink won't you?

I got some American beer especially for you." Fred was a little unsure, as it was still in the middle of the morning. However, he quickly caught on that refusal was not an option and took the attitude of, "When in Rome, do as the Romans." So, he gladly surrendered, and the stage was set for a wonderful morning. As she settled down in her chair, she began by saying "C'mere 'till I tell you." Over the course of the next three hours, Fred was treated to story after story of Auntie Betty's upbringing in Northern Ireland.

Storytelling is part of Irish DNA. Indeed, there is a unique word in the Irish language for a storyteller, *seanchaí* (pronounced shan-a-KEY). Seanchaí is not just the word for a storyteller but for something richer—it means "the keeper of a tradition." They had a critical role is passing on the history, myths, and traditions of the country during a time when knowledge was through the word of mouth. The seanchaí went from town to town, meeting in people's houses and reciting ancient legends such as Cú Chulainn (pronounced KOO-hullan), known for his strength and power, or Fionn mac Cumhaill (pronounced fin-mac-KOOL), the leader of the Fianna warriors.

The seanchaí were a major source of entertainment. People would gather around a fire and be enthralled with the stories. Seanchaí had a skill in making the everyday, ordinary events interesting.

Stories of the baker, the bus driver, or a funeral were relived with a little embellishment to add to the entertainment value;

Mark Twain once said, "Never let the truth get in the way of a good story."

The pub was the natural progression of this history. The early seanchaí visited people's homes and local villagers gathered to be entertained. In time, these homes, known for their warm welcome and good craíc, naturally turned into pubs. The owner of the house simply put his name on a sign and hung it outside the house. This tradition can still be seen today; the names of various pubs are simply the family name.

Figure 6.1 P. Egan Bar, Moate, Co. Westmeath, Ireland.

Figure 6.2 S. Kelly's Pub, Ballymahon, Co. Longford, Ireland.

The layout of the pub also has been influenced by the tradition of the seanchaí; many have a fireplace with lots of room for gatherings around the fire. Center stage, of course, would be the seanchaí telling their story.

Many Irish pubs also have area called the snug. The snug was an intimate space with walled dividers to keep it private. It provided space for groups to share tales and stories. At first, the snugs allowed women to go to the pub and have a drink. Before this, women were not allowed in pubs, as they were the exclusive domain of men. However, that situation changed, and women moved from the snug to the main bar.

The snugs were not removed, as they allowed people who wanted to remain private to have a drink. These people included the local priest or gardaí (police), or those who needed some privacy for a deal they were negotiating. If you have ever seen the series "Peaky Blinkers," you see the snug used often by the Shelby gang in the Garrison pub, where they wheel and deal out of the view of others.

Figure 6.3 The snug in Doheny & Nesbitt Pub, Dublin, Ireland. (Image used with permission @dublinsnugs Instagram)

It is perhaps the barman and owner—always ready to engage in a conversation with those in the bar—who has inherited the role of the seanchaí. I know my father was always ready to tell a story or draw one out of others. I remember him doubled over in laughter recounting different stories and customers laughing with tears in their eyes.

At the age of twelve, I was allowed to collect the empty glasses and wash them out. This privilege allowed me to listen into the conversations at the pub and hear their stories.

There was a story of Peter, a regular of the pub, who went on a day trip with his wife, Shelia, to Scotland by ferry for a friend's engagement celebration. Peter recounted how the party was held at the local pub and the craíc was brilliant. Of course, the beer flowed, and he admitted that he might have had a little too much. At the end of the evening, he remembered the plan was to take the last ferry home so they would not have to spend the night. He made it to the ferry on time and after it docked, he took the short walk home and collapsed in bed and fell into a deep sleep.

He was suddenly woken up the next morning by the sound of the phone ringing. He had a splitting headache. He answered the phone and was surprised to hear a Scottish policeman on the other end. His heart began to beat faster as he tried to remember what he might have happened the night before. Indeed, he had little memory of how he made it back home at all.

"Are you Peter McHenry?"

"Aye, I am."

"And are you married to Shelia McHenry?"

"Aye, I am."

"Well, we found a woman sitting on a street bench here this morning. She had celebrated a little too hard and sure, she lost her purse and she could not get home. We took her in, and she told us to call you."

As the veil of the previous evening lifted, Peter suddenly realized that Shelia was not beside him. Indeed, the more he thought about it, he did not remember her on the ferry on the way back, nor her walking with him home. Then the terrible reality dawned on him—he had left her in Scotland. Peter realized this was way worse than being in trouble with the police. His voice was now shaking.

"OK, tell her I'll take the next ferry over." As he listened to the policeman telling his wife what he said, he could hear her muffled voice and the policeman laughing.

"What did she say?" Peter asked, almost not wanting to hear the answer.

"She told me to tell you that you might as well bring a coffin with you when you come over, as you will need it for the journey home."

Peter took the ferry over and the even longer ferry back, in total silence. At the end of the story, everyone burst into laughter. They were not laughing at Peter, but laughing with him. It came from the realization that it could have happened to anyone there. As Peter told the story, we all could feel his anxiety on the way to pick up Shelia and the silence of that ferry home.

The Leader As A Seanchaí

The leader is also called to be a seanchaí. Now, at first sight, the worlds of a leader and a storyteller might seem very different; management and leadership are driven by data and reason, while storytelling seems to be another world which is soft, emotional, irrational, and a little childish. However, nothing could be further from the truth. At the core of leadership is the task of persuasion. It involves winning the hearts and minds of others and gaining their trust. In many ways, the CEO must also be the CSO (Chief Storytelling Officer).

Leaders today operate at an incredibly busy pace; they are bombarded with different messages and live with immense pressure to make quick decisions. The world in which they live and breathe is becoming more complex. Communication seems to have been reduced to the smallest soundbite. However, if a leader is looking to express ideas in a dynamic way that will be memorable and impactful, then storytelling is an essential skillset. Why? Janis Forman, who has extensively researched the impact of storytelling on communication, explains. "Humans crave narrative, and the use of story builds a narrative for topics that goes deeper and lives longer in a person's psyche than most any other form of communication."[23]

Why is it that storytelling is such a powerful tool for leaders? Let me point to two recent findings in neuroscience that shed light on this phenomenon.

1. We Use Stories To Make Meaning

The ability to read is a very recent occurrence. When the colonists in America revolted against King George, it was thought that only half of the population was literate. The oldest written language we know is Sumerian, and it dates to around 7,000 years ago. However, it is thought that humans shared stories with each other at least 100,000 years ago. Stories were a way of communicating lifesaving information, such as, "Don't go there, there is a dangerous animal," or, "Don't eat this, or you will die." Storytelling is so embedded into our being that, in many ways, it is how we make meaning of our reality.

Every five seconds our senses gather eleven million pieces of data. We are only capable of registering forty of them and processing seven of them! How do we deal with all this data, and which data points do we choose to process? The noted neuroscientist Antonio Demasio points to storytelling as the medium we have chosen to express what is relevant (2012).[24] While the brain is constantly trying to make meaning from all this data it is consuming, it chooses what is important for our survival and then tells a story about it.

Even if we have gaps in the basic information, we find it hard to resist not filling these gaps so that we can make sense of it. Kendall Haven has a wonderful way of showing this phenomenon.[25] Take the following two sentences spoken by two different people:

Person #1: Where's John?

Person #2: Well … I didn't want to say anything, but … I saw a green Volkswagen parked in front of Carol's.

Now stop and take a few moments to consider what is happening in this situation. What story did you come up with in your head?

I have done this exercise with many audiences and the answers they come up with are incredibly creative. For some, it points to Carol having an affair or to John's murdered body lying in the trunk of the Volkswagen. At the end of the discussion, people want to know what the correct answer is. Of course, there is no correct answer. These are two sentences that, for all intents and purposes, have nothing to do with each other. However, our drive for meaning makes us want to make connections even where there appears to be none. We want a story about what has happened or is happening.

As a side note, this concept is also incredibly important for the workplace. How often do we make decisions and rush to assumptions when we do not have any information to back them up? This tendency comes, in part, from an innate desire within us to make connections and complete the story.

We always turn to stories to explain what is happening to us or those around us. Just listen to the stories that are constantly going on in your head.

"Betty is always on time; how come she's half an hour late?"

"John always has coffee in the morning; I wonder why he didn't today."

As storytellers, we're constantly looking for what is happening beneath the surface of reality; it shows us how we are interpreting reality and highlights what is important to us.

2. Story Creates Connection By Fully Engaging Us

With the onset of new technology such as FMRI (functional magnetic resonance imaging) scans, we now understand what happens in the brain when we listen to a story, and it is truly fascinating. We'd expect the language-processing parts of the brain, the Broca and the Wernicke, to be active. What was totally unexpected was the activity in the motor, sensory, and olfactory cortexes depending on what was said. Researchers from Emory University have shown that when participants were read sentences such as, "The singer had a velvet voice," and "He had leathery hands," their sensory cortexes were activated along with the language parts of the brain. When they heard

"John grasped the object," and "Pablo kicked the ball," their motor cortexes were activated.[26]

This simply amazing finding shows that we are not just hearing the words, we are actually experiencing them, as if we were the central character in all the actions. It is as if we are hearing the velvety voice and grasping the object or kicking the ball. A story is an amazing simulator, and when we hear it, we are transported into another reality.

What's more, research by Paul Zak showed that when we hear emotional stories, it increases our level of oxytocin.[27] This is significant because oxytocin is also called the "cuddle hormone." Oxytocin is directly involved in our feelings of connection and trust. The higher the levels of oxytocin, the greater the feelings of connection and trust.

With this connection in mind, it is clear that storytelling can be a powerful tool for leaders. What are some practical steps for using storytelling in the workplace?

1. Build A Story Vault

I offer a training in presentation skills, and one of the things I remind anyone who attends is that few of them are aware they are sitting on a goldmine. Their goldmines are the life experiences of everyone in the room and the stories that flow from those experiences. It's as if every person has their own Fort Knox full of bullion. Unfortunately, the storytelling gold is locked away for most of us, and never sees the light of day. One of the most important steps anyone who wants to incorporate storytelling into their leadership can take is to mine their own experience. What stories come to mind from your years at work, your leadership challenges and successes? You can also expand this story hoard to include stories from growing up, going to school, and life in general. At first, it can be difficult to come up with many stories, but when you set your mind to it, you will be amazed at what comes up. I also suggest keeping a story journal to jot down what comes to mind.

2. What Is The Message I Wish To Communicate?

If there is one common struggle that I see among most communicators: a clear message. It is much easier in talk on and on than to have laser clarity in what you are going to say. Once you are clear on the message you wish to communicate, the next question should be, "What delivery vehicle will I use to deliver the message?" More often than not, you should consider a story. Why? Because it is memorable. If you stop people coming out of any meeting or presentation and ask them what they remember about the presentation, more often than not they will recall a story that was told. People will remember a story before any statistics or trends cited. Indeed, I always encourage leaders who have statistics in their presentations or talks to try and embody those statistics in a story. It is a much better way of bringing those numbers to life.

3. Where Is The Struggle?

All stories need a struggle built into them. Struggle makes a story interesting. Perhaps it's a change that is needed in a change-resistant culture, a competitor who is outmaneuvering you, market conditions that look bleak in the coming year, or an invisible virus leading to a global pandemic forcing abrupt changes. Michael Hauge, who consults with Hollywood directors on how to make their stories more powerful, says that the goal of all stories is to elicit emotion, and he contends that emotion grows out of conflict.[28] In the story of Peter, there was the epic struggle of leaving his wife behind and the tension of not knowing what would happen when he picked her up.

4. You're Not The Hero

Every story also needs a hero who overcomes conflict. However, you should never be the hero of your own story. Let's face it, if you have all the answers to every struggle you have gone through, how will people relate to your story and be moved by it? Instead, try and make others the hero. Focus on the lessons they have taught you. If the company is preparing for a challenging year, shine light on employees who stepped up in the past. Jonah Sachs comments, "One of the main reasons we listen to stories is to create a deeper belief in ourselves."[29] When a story moves us to believe we have the power to overcome a challenge, we have engaged and motivated others, which is much more powerful that showing how great we are.

5. Keep It Simple

Stories do not have to be long and involved. Indeed, the sign of a great storyteller is one who knows how much color to add without dragging the story down with superfluous details. Keep close to the central struggle of the story and only veer from this lane if you think doing so will add to the central premise or struggle.

Conflict lies at the core of great storytelling. Conflict is part of life and the daily reality of work. However, we are not always skilled in dealing with it. The center of many coaching sessions I've led with executives examined a conflict they were having and assessing how they were dealing with that conflict. Let's look at the reality of conflict in the next chapter.

Lesson 4 Inventory

Reflect on the statement and how you typically "show up" at work. Think of examples in your experience. Place an "X" along the continuum that best reflects you.

I have a rich number of stories which I use when I communicate.	Almost Never True	Almost Always True
I often struggle to make my communication succinct.	Almost Never True	Almost Always True
I am often surprised to find that people haven't understood what I've said.	Almost Never True	Almost Always True
Before I communicate, I think about what the person needs to know, and how best to convey it.	Almost Never True	Almost Always True

Lesson 4 Toolbox

Please visit www.leadershiplessonsfromthepub.com/toolbox

1. Creating A Story Vault. (Activity).
2. Story Questions (Worksheet).
3. Elements Of A Great Story (Activity).
4. How To Develop Trust And Confidence In The Workplace? (Video).

CHAPTER 7

Like A Bridge Over Troubled Water

LESSON #5: *You Are Called To Be A Bridge, Not A Wall*

very year, our grade school would organize an educational outing. When I was in eighth grade, the trip was to the north Antrim coast, a majestic stretch of coastline with scenic drives and the world famous Giant's Causeway. However, it was a visit to another iconic spot, the Carrick-a-Rede rope bridge, that truly caught my attention. The rope bridge was built in 1755 to connect the Carrick-a-Rede island with the mainland. The water around the island was rich with salmon and the bridge was built to carry boxes of salmon from the island. The bridge is sixty-six feet wide and ninety-eight feet above the rocks and ocean below.

As someone who has always being afraid of heights, walking across it was a truly toe-curling experience. I still remember that day—it was sunny, but the wind was blowing, and the bridge was gently swaying. I can plainly say that if it was not for the peer pressure of twenty-five other classmates on the trip, I would not have even stepped a foot on the bridge. However, I mustered up all the courage I had and made it to the other side, only to be horrified with the realization that had not dawned on me before—this would be a round trip; there was no way back to the mainland other than returning over the bridge.

Figure 7.1 Carrick-a-Rede island and its famous rope bridge.

Figure 7.2 Looking down from the Carrick-a-Rede rope bridge.

As part of our schoolwork in the week following, we did different projects exploring bridges and their importance in connecting people and building peace and prosperity. How interesting, therefore, at that exact time, only seventy-five miles away in Belfast, walls were being built to separate the Protestant and Catholic communities as tensions escalated due to the terrible bombings and violence of The Troubles which began in 1968. These walls, which eventually stretched for twenty-one miles, were euphemistically called "peace walls."

Figure 7.3 A section of the peace wall dividing communities – Luc V. de Zeeuw.

One of the core choices we have in the face of any conflict is to ask ourselves the simple question, "Am I going to build a bridge or a wall?" After the bombing of the pub, it would have been so easy for my parents to wallow in anger and seek revenge, or to retreat and take care of their wounds. My father's response was, "Watch me build again." He built bridges.

In Northern Ireland in the mid-1970s, these peace walls segregated communities. There were Protestant pubs and Catholic pubs. However, in our village, we were the only pub, and it was mixed; both Catholics and Protestants drank side by side. It never really struck me how extraordinary this was.

Although I was raised a Catholic, I had many Protestant friends, and even went to a Protestant grade school for a while.

My father's philosophy was always to include people, to widen the circle. It was a belief that cost him and our family a great deal. People of violence only sought to erect walls and create deeper division. We now know the reason our bar was bombed by the IRA was because of the fact that Protestants, some of whom were off-duty policemen, drank in the pub. Indeed, my dad even received threats to stop serving Protestants or suffer the consequences. In the face of this pressure, the easy course would have been to retreat and build walls; however, it takes courage to build a bridge.

In our pub, all the tools needed for bridge-building were evident each evening. Most importantly, we had the ability to listen to another person. Growing up in Northern Ireland, we were all fed the gospel of difference. Each side of the conflict had its own history and traditions, and each had its own story. Each believed that the only right interpretation of history was its own. This mutual certainty only highlighted and emphasized everything that was different, and ignored commonalities.

However, in the pub, talk turned to the struggles of life, relationships, and work. These conversations were about shared experiences and how alike we all are. I remember John would sometimes come in for a drink in the evening. After settling down he would often remark that his wife was "Doing his head in," a wonderful Irish expression which signified that she was annoying him. He would tell his tale of woe and the others would offer words of advice from experience and John would go home armed with a few new strategies.

It is often said that if pubs did not exist, Ireland would have to dramatically increase the number of psychologists and psychiatrists to cope with the loss of spaces where people could destress and talk things out.

That does not mean that life in the pub was always rosy or that conflicts never escalated.

Sometimes, tensions boiled over and a fight ensued, or a customer would continually aggravate others with comments. In these cases, my father might have no resort but to "bar" the person from the pub. To bar someone meant that the offending customer was not allowed to come back into the pub for a period; a type of time-out.

My father hated to bar people because he hated to exclude anyone. Before he would bar someone, he would always have a word with them privately and ask for the offending behavior to stop. Most often, the customer would apologize and promise that his behavior would change. Often, they were just not aware that their words or behaviors had upset anyone. If the behavior continued, then they would be barred for a period of a few weeks to a month.

At the end of their time-out, the customer would return, and my father would have another conversation with them and seek assurances that the lesson had been learned and the behavior would change. Occasionally, an apology to a customer who had been offended was required. For most, that was all it took and there never was another incident.

However, if a customer's behavior was dangerous, they were barred for life. I remember one morning seeing my father with a swollen face. "What the hell happened to you?" I asked. My father replied, "Some eejit (idiot) got angry when his half-finished drink was taken at the end of the night after he had gone to the bathroom. He grabbed me by the tie and head-butted me." "What did you do?" I asked. "I barred him for life, good riddance to him. He has been poisoning the place for too long."

In the end, it was not about appeasing the offending customer but rather maintaining the craíc for the rest of the customers. No sooner had he barred someone, would he receive thanks from a whole host of other people.

Of course, conflict is not only part of the life of a pub, it also part of the life of any organization. All leaders have to manage and effectively deal with conflict. Because of the leader's unique role, how they manage conflict will have a ripple-down effect on the organization as a whole. While it's hard to put a figure on how much time a leader spends managing conflict, research by Howard Guttman indicated that leaders can spend 24 percent of their time resolving conflicts.[30] This is a huge amount of time and energy. It's vital, therefore, for leaders to understand their approach to conflict and how that approach may differ from others'.

Each of us has a conflict story—as we grew up, we all developed attitudes and approaches to conflict. This development was influenced by the example of those around us and by some of our basic needs. It is very powerful to spend some time and review our lives, see how we tend to deal with conflict, and examine some of the lessons we learned growing up. For me, growing up with violence all around, I saw conflict as something to be feared. Conflict was something that could potentially get out of control and hurt people. Conflict was a bad thing. It is not surprising, therefore, that conflict has caused me a lot of anxiety.

Often, our approach to conflict is driven by a deeper interpersonal need. For me, it was a need for harmony and the need to be liked. As I review my life, I see patterns of avoiding conflict at work and at home to maintain harmony, and not risking something getting out of control which would put me into disfavor. What is your conflict story? The first step for leaders to effectively lead through conflict is to know their own unique patterns and default patterns.

One of the most helpful models for this exploration is the Thomas Kilmann Conflict Mode Instrument (TKI). This tool assesses an individual's typical behavior in conflict and helps them understand approaches that might be more effective in a particular situation. It was instrumental in helping understand my own approach to conflict and helped me grow and develop different methods to managing conflict. I have used it with many clients over the years who have found it equally enlightening each time.

TKI lays out five different styles of handling conflict. Each style is a combination of how assertive and cooperative we are in a conflict situation. Assertiveness means the degree you will try to satisfy your own concerns during a conflict. Cooperativeness means the degree to which you will try and satisfy the concerns of another person.

Let's review the five styles and see if you can detect your preferred approach to conflict. It is also useful to note that there is no one style that is inherently best, but a particular conflict approach might be more useful than another, depending on the situation. A skilled leader, while more comfortable in one approach, can learn how to use the others to handle conflict in a new way.

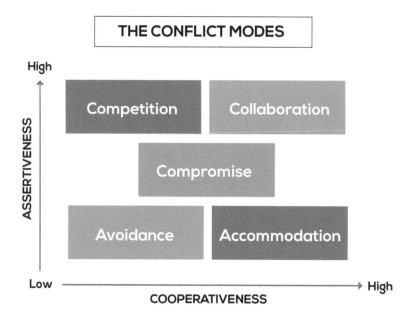

Figure 7.4 TKI Profile Model (More information can be found at www.kilmanndiagnostics.com).

1. Avoidance (Low Assertiveness And Low Cooperativeness)

If this is your style, you don't try to satisfy your own concerns or the concerns of another person. You either sidestep the conflict or stay away from it entirely. While you may perceive this tactic as being diplomatic, the issue continues to boil and can have an impact on the wider organization. However, there are times when this style can be useful. If emotions are running very high and any conversation will be unproductive, it is good to take a break so people can cool down. If the conflict involves two other people and they are capable of solving the issue, as a leader, you may choose not to insert yourself.

2. Accommodation (Low Assertiveness And High Cooperativeness)

At the core of this mode is the yielding of one party to protect and preserve the relationship. You are willing to sacrifice your needs for the benefit of the other person. This is my default style. Of course, the risk here is that you let other people walk over you and you never assert your own needs. However, this style can be useful in certain situations. If the issue at the core of the conflict is more important to the other person than it is to you, it may well be advantageous to yield. You may also realize you are wrong and decide to be accommodating. Finally, you may accommodate others even if you know they are wrong, as a developmental process, so they can learn from their mistakes.

3. Compromise (Mid-Level Assertiveness And Mid-Level Cooperativeness)

With the compromise mode, both parties in the conflict are willing to sacrifice some of their concerns and be content partially satisfying their own interests. The danger of this mode is that others can con you into compromising more. However, it can be useful when you are at a standstill with someone and there needs to be movement. This mode can help by offering a temporary solution.

4. Collaboration (High Assertiveness And High Cooperativeness)

This mode is an attempt to solve the issue at hand by meeting the interests of all parties. It is important to note that this style takes a lot of time and energy from everyone involved. I often find that collaboration is a buzzword in leadership; however, I do not think there is an appreciation for how much time it really takes. This style is best used when the solution is going to have a significant impact on the people involved, and the concerns of both parties are too important to be ignored.

5. Competition (High Assertiveness And Low Cooperativeness)

In this style, you impose your solution on the other party, and with this tactic, your interests are met at the cost of the other person's interests. In this approach, there is a willingness to sacrifice the relationship. This approach is best used when there is an emergency and decisive action is required.

What is important to note is that there is no one-size-fits-all approach to conflict. Skilled leaders are able to assess the situation and determine what approach might work best. This assessment can take some work up-front, but the payoff is well worth it. Below are some important questions to reflect upon:

- What are the core issues involved in this conflict?

- Am I missing any information?

- What am I looking for, and why is it important to me or the organization?

- What is the other person looking for, and why is that important to them or the organization?

- What points of view do we share in common?

- Is this the right time to for me to get involved?

This final question can be very revealing. In coaching conversations, I often hear leaders who are being brought into a situation by two others who are in conflict. The problem with getting involved too quickly is that there is a danger they will place the burden of the conflict on your shoulders; you become responsible for the resolution. Sometimes, it is best not to get involved, but reaffirm the other parties' ability to resolve the issue.

It's also very important to be aware of emotions that might be generated in any meeting or discussion, and how you might deal with them. During the training I offer on emotional skills, attendees get an opportunity to simulate a difficult workplace conversation they need to have. Another attendee takes on the role of the other person in the conversation. As part of the pre-work for the conversation, we speak about the potential emotions that might arise (anger, fear, or disgust), what emotional trigger buttons might be pressed in the conversation, how we could notice them in ourselves (physiological signals or body language), or in the other person (facial expressions, body language, voice, or content). This preparation, I find, is often overlooked. When it comes to potentially difficult conversations, we find it natural to go over the words we might use in our head, but most of the time, we forgot to think about the emotions that will be stirred and how we will manage them.

Finally, it is important to realize conflict is not inherently bad. Rather, conflict is an inevitable situation arising from the fact that, as individuals, we have different needs, beliefs, and concerns. How we deal with these differences can be in a heathy or unhealthy manner. The more skilled a leader is in these different approaches, the better able they are to resolve issues and see that everyone is respected and heard. This approach is not easy, and at times it takes courage and resilience—which forms the core of our next chapter.

Lesson 5 Inventory

Reflect on the statement and how you typically "show up" at work. Think of examples in your experience. Place an "X" along the continuum that best reflects you.

	Almost Never True	Almost Always True
I find conflicts challenging and exhilarating; I enjoy the battle of wits that usually follows.		
I prefer to keep the peace than get what I want.		
When I find myself in an argument, I usually say very little and try to leave as soon as possible.		
To break deadlocks, I usually meet people halfway.		
I can tell if someone is upset or annoyed with me.		

Lesson 5 Toolbox

Please visit www.leadershiplessonsfromthepub.com/toolbox

1. Assessments And Assertions.
2. How To Prepare For A Difficult Conversation.
3. 7 Ways To Manage Feedback At Work.
4. How To Manage Conflict And Disagreements With Colleagues.

CHAPTER 8

When Words Fail, Music Speaks

LESSON #6: *You Are Called To Hold Space*

Less than two years after the bombing of our pub in 1973, our new pub opened and Dad took the opportunity to make two changes. The first was expanding the bar lounge, with a large dance floor that could accommodate live music. Second, he built a new house separate from the pub at the other end of the parking lot. Should the pub ever experience a bombing or fire again, we would not be out of our home as well.

I spent most every weekend of my teenage years working in the pub and enjoying the live music. In the 1970s and 1980s, the who's who of our local music scene came and played there, including such acts as the Dew Drops, Snowbird, the Playboys, and Frank Chisum and the Fashion. Frank Chisum also did an Elvis impersonation that always drew a large crowd. Perhaps the biggest star, however, was Philomena Begley, a local country singer who had people up singing and dancing all night.

Figure 8.1 Strabane Chronicle Newspaper ad for upcoming Ballymagorry Arms entertainment August, 1976.

I remember seeing her in the pub one night. I was sitting next to my mother who loved her music. Philomena Begley started singing "The Way Old Friends Do,"[31] originally recorded by ABBA. When she sang, you could feel the emotion of each word, and in that moment, something happened, which only music can do. It touched the hearts and tapped the unexpressed feelings of those gathered. As I looked at my mother, I could see her smile and a tear roll down her face. That tear contained loss and sorrow, but also a hope for a better day.

You and I can share the silence
Finding comfort together
The way old friends do

And after fights and words of violence
We make up with each other
The way old friends do

Times of joy and times of sorrow
We will always see it through
Oh, I don't care what comes tomorrow
We can face it together
The way old friends do

Music has always been the center of Irish life, and in particular, the center of the pub. Traditional Irish music has its origins in the east. The Celts came from central Europe around 500 BC. While they settled throughout Europe, it was in Ireland, Scotland, Brittany in northwestern France, and Galicia in Spain that Celtic culture thrived. If you listen to the music of these places, you will hear parallel melodies and combinations of similar-sounding instruments in each.

Many pubs have musical evenings when people from the local community bring their instruments and play. It's a nonstop celebration of sound and storytelling making sure the evening is full of craíc. It's hard not to listen and feel part of something that is bigger than you. However, it's not just about the music; it's the warm atmosphere, a place to belong through the good and the bad.

Managing a pub during the years of The Troubles in Northern Ireland was no easy feat. It took a tremendous amount of resilience on my family's part. Yet, the pub played an important role in creating a space where people could go and draw resilience from each other. The pub was able to hold the breadth of human emotions—celebrating in good times, and acknowledging and being present in the bad times. In many ways, it was a sacred space.

Music was best able to put into words what was below the surface. It is not surprising that recent research, specifically in conflict zones, has pointed to the presence of humor and joy, the ability to express loss, close human connections, and a sense of optimism and hope as key elements in the development of resilience.[32,33] I saw all of these elements in the pub, and music was at the heart of their expression.

Celebration And Joy

Despite the growing violence on the streets during The Troubles, life went on. The pub offered a haven in many ways where cares could be temporarily forgotten, life was celebrated, and laughter was enjoyed. There was never a shortage of jokes or a funny commentary about what was happening in the village or on television. In many ways, such celebration was an act of resistance—to keep the laughter, the joy, keep singing the song, and keep the melody going, as did this traditional pub song, "Beer, Beer, Beer."

A long time ago, way back in history,
When all there was to drink was nothin' but cups of tea.
Along came a man by the name of Charlie Mops,
And he invented a wonderful drink and he made it out of hops.

He must have been an admiral, a sultan, or a king,
And to his praises we shall always sing.
Look what he has done for us, he's filled us up with cheer!
Lord bless Charlie Mops, the man who invented beer beer beer
Tiddly beer beer beer.

Loss

Over 3,500 people were killed and over 50,000 people were injured in the years of The Troubles. There was hardly a single person who did not know someone who was injured or killed; so much loss. How do you bring that grief to the surface? It's not easy in general, and of course, every loss is unique to the individual. Yet, in Northern Ireland, our personal losses were also part of the collective loss, which included the loss of family and friends in the violence, of homes and businesses, economic stability, and childhood.

Few have captured the emotion of the loss of childhood as American folk singer Nancy Griffith who was deeply touched after a visit to Belfast. Her haunting voice only served to bring out the lyrics of a deep sadness of the impact of violence on a whole generation of youth in "It's A Hard Life Wherever You Go."[34]

I am a backseat driver from America
They drive to the left on Falls Road
The man at the wheel's name is Seamus
We pass a child on the corner he knows
And Seamus says, "Now, what chance has that kid got?"
And I say from the back, "I don't know."
He says, "There's barbed wire at all of these exits
And there ain't no place in Belfast for that kid to go."

It's a hard life
It's a hard life
It's a very hard life
It's a hard life wherever you go
If we poison our children with hatred
Then, the hard life is all that they'll know
And there ain't no place in Belfast for
These kids to go

On August 15, 1998, the worst single tragedy of The Troubles happened in Omagh, where I was born. A car bomb went off in a crowded street, injuring 220 people and killing twenty-nine. The bombing was carried out by an IRA splinter group opposed to the ceasefire that had been declared by the IRA. A week later, the town center was packed with people for a memorial service. How do you put into words that loss? For me, the nearest was a song sung that afternoon by Juliet Turner, a local singer, whose raw vocal delivery gave voice to the rawness that every person gathered there felt inside in "Broken Things" written by Julie Miller.

You can have my heart
But it isn't new
It's been used and broken
And only comes in blue
It's been down a long road
And it got dirty on the way
If I give it to you will you make it clean
And wash the pain away

Hope And Optimism

My mother loved the music of Phil Coulter, a masterful songwriter from Northern Ireland. In particular, she adored "The Town I Loved So Well." The song took the listener from growing up as a child in a town's streets to the onset of The Troubles with the tanks and bombs to the optimism of the final verse that there would be a new day for the city. I heard it many times played at the pub, by different music groups who each gave it their unique take.

Now the music's gone but I still carry on
For their spirit's been bruised never broken
They will not forget for their hearts are a set
On tomorrow and peace once again
For what's done is done and what's won is won
And what's lost is lost and gone forever
I can only pray for a bright brand new day
In the town I loved so well

Both my parents had every reason to be pessimistic about everything that was happening around them. Yet within them was an unquenchable hope that things would be better. My mother drew from a deep religious faith which told her that light was more powerful than darkness. My father had a faith in the goodness of human beings and their ability to get along and make peace. Of all the character traits I have picked up from my parents, it is these I am most grateful for. I have a rock-solid belief in the goodness of humanity and the faith to endure whatever darkness surrounds me, for I know that light will come.

Creating Space For Resilience To Grow

The terrain that leaders work in today is extremely difficult. Rapid change, complexity, and greater competition are the norm; to survive long-term in such an environment one needs to be resilient. I think one of the most beautiful images for a leader is that of Ben Zander, the world-renowned conductor of the Boston Philharmonic Orchestra, who notes that the conductor is the only one in an orchestra who does not play an instrument.[35] However, the conductor's role is to draw out the best in each musician and to create a space in which each can thrive.

It is the same with leadership. A leader's task is to create a space in which each employee can thrive. It is clear that there is a direct correlation between this and higher job satisfaction, greater job commitment, improved feelings of connectedness, and better job performance outcomes.[36]

How then can a leader develop resilience within the organization? Three different elements are critically important for building resilience, all of which were clearly present in the pub as well.

1. Laughter And Fun

One of the ways to reduce the amount of stress within an organization by seeing humor even in the midst of difficult times. Most work cultures are sober environments and organizations in which there is a high level of anxiety are often very serious and lack an ability to laugh at themselves. Eric Tsytsylin comments that most working adults are "in the midst of a laughter drought."[37] It seems as we get older, we laugh less often. Babies laugh 400 times a day on average, yet those over thirty-five only laugh fifteen times a day. We also laugh significantly less during the week.

The link between laughter and resilience is clear. Laughter helps a person gain a different perspective on a situation and become more relaxed. It enables us to release some tension and anxiety. Skilled leaders know just when a serious situation needs to be lightened. Making a funny comment can diffuse a tense situation.

Good humor in the workplace does not begin with the words, "Did you hear the one about . . . ?" Rather, humor is the ability to shine light on a situation and see the funny side of it. Often, it can be poking fun at yourself.

Why does humor work so well? It's science. Robert Provine notes that laughter is the most contagious of all the emotions.[38] It is the most direct communication between two people. Laughter also sparks the release of oxytocin, a hormone that facilitates social bonding, increases trust, and quickens self-disclosure.

2. Optimism

The link between resilience and optimism has been researched widely. Almost unanimously, studies point to the positive relationship between optimism and increased well-being, higher levels of resilience, and lower levels of stress.

Those who are most resilient are able to explain a situation in optimistic terms, helping them to avoid falling into helplessness. They tend to look at a setback as something that is temporary and changeable:

> "This will resolve itself quickly . . ."

> "I can readjust and make it better . . ."

In contrast, those who are more pessimistic in nature can look at the same setbacks and see them as something that is permanent and immutable:

> "There is nothing I can do about it . . ."

> "Things will never be any different . . ."

Martin Seligman, a professor of positive psychology at the University of Pennsylvania, has shown that optimism is not something that is fixed within us; it can be expanded.[39]

At the core of building optimism is emotional reappraisal, the ability to change the way that we think and feel about events that happen to us. When something happens, it generates thoughts and emotions within us. Those who are more optimistic are able to reappraise the situation and modify their perception of what is happening, which can lead to a different emotional response. I live in Washington DC, which vies with Los Angeles for the worst traffic in the US. When I am driving, a person will sometimes cut me off, causing me to press my brakes. When this happens, I can feel my body tense, my hand grips the steering wheel, and I think, "What an a******!" If I can try to come up with alternative reasons for their behavior in that moment (they have an emergency to get to, they have to get to the bathroom) I can begin to lessen the severity of my response and have different thoughts about it.

As leaders, we should also be more self-aware and challenge any of the stories we make up about a situation or event. So often our stories are based on false or incomplete information. As we saw in Chapter 6, it hard to resist filling in the gaps of an incomplete story. Our stories can also assume negative intent. For example, Tom is late for a meeting. Sometimes our story can be, "Doesn't Tom know how important this meeting is? I guess it's not that important for him. How disrespectful he is being to me and the others!" That may be one explanation, but there are others.

One practice helpful in this situation is to try and come up with three other explanations. What is important is to notice our immediate negative judgment and how we jumped to this conclusion. Sometimes when I am working with clients, they will tell me a story of something that happened to them. If I can see that it is riddled in assumptions, I will ask them, "If you told this story in court, is there enough evidence for a conviction?" Often there is not, and it helps separate what I know to be fact from what was added without any evidence.

3. Holding Space For Difficult Emotions

The optimism that is mentioned above is not a Pollyannaish optimism that overlooks any negative or difficult situations. Rather, it is a realistic optimism which has space to acknowledge setbacks and difficulties. The emotion of sadness often goes unrecognized in the workplace. Sadness, in all its different intensities, has a common universal trigger—loss. It can be the loss of a loved one or the loss of a physical thing. In the workplace, loss takes on many different dimensions: the loss of a promotion, the loss of a sales contract, the loss of an office space. These losses can generate many different emotions and the feeling that things are happening to us, over which we have no control.

I find that, as a culture, the US does a terrible job of acknowledging loss. When a loved one dies, we know that an impacted person will need some time to grieve. However, in many—if not most—work situations, we expect that grief to be worked out by the time the person returns to work. Most companies' bereavement polices only allow for a few days away from work. When the bereaved person returns, other employees may be nervous about bringing up the death for fear of causing hurt. This silence, in turn, can create an awkward environment where no one is talking about the elephant in the room.

Of course, sadness and grief are not that tidy. We all deal with loss differently. For some, the emotional impact is immediate, while for others, months can pass before it is felt. I like the image of waves to express what loss is like. Some days we are fine, and then on others, the waves come upon us and can be triggered by anything—music, a memory, a smell, or something that connects us to our loved one.

Even less recovery time is extended to those who are experiencing the loss of promotion or a contract that did not come through. It's vital that we acknowledge those losses. There is only so much we can suppress before it comes out in other forms, such as passive-aggressiveness or negativity.

Otto Scharmer, senior lecturer at MIT and founding chair of the Presencing Institute, said that "Holding space is the single most important leadership capacity going forward."[40] "Holding space" means the ability of a leader to not impose an outcome or rush a situation, but to sit with ambiguity and be open to the direction in which they should move when it emerges.

As a leader, it's incredibly important to model that you create space for loss in your own life. Don't be afraid to talk about the losses you've experienced in the workplace. Go from there to hold the space for others to mention their losses as well. When done well, this practice can enable deeper connection and support, key ingredients of resilience.

It's clear that this call to hold space feels different from the fast pace of modern business. Yet this pace is burning people out at alarming rates. That burnout calls for a new way of thinking about time and energy—and the pub has a lot to teach us.

Lesson 6 Inventory

Reflect on the comment and how you typically "show up" at work. Think of examples in your experience. Place an "X" along the continuum that best reflects you.

I remain optimistic even when things are not going my way?	Almost Never True	Almost Always True
I maintain a good sense of humor even in very serious situations?	Almost Never True	Almost Always True
I can remain comfortable when others become very emotional.	Almost Never True	Almost Always True
I can sense when people have something troubling them.	Almost Never True	Almost Always True

Lesson 6 Toolbox

Please visit www.leadershiplessonsfromthepub.com/toolbox

1. Boost Your Optimism.
2. Dealing With Strong Emotions.
3. Finding Humor Exercise.
4. How To Positively Influence Others In The Workplace.

CHAPTER 9

Time After Time

LESSON #7: *You Have The Power To Be A Thin Place*

When I was in my fourth year of seminary in Dublin, my best friend, Kevin, and I decided to help organize a walk for peace over the Dublin mountains to the small village of Glendalough. Full of excitement, we jumped in headfirst in getting others in the seminary to take part. In total, the walk was just over thirty-one miles with a stop overnight at the Glencree Centre for Peace, almost halfway to our goal.

At 7 a.m. on October 3, 1989, 200 brave souls began the trek. At first, all was fun, as we got to meet new people. We made it to Glencree, tired and sore. The next day, we set of at 8 a.m. on a brilliantly sunny day. Although we had sixteen miles to go, we were confident we would make it.

However, by 11 a.m., that confidence had turned into doubt and pain. All I saw before me were huge hills. As if to add insult to injury, by noon, our sunny day had changed into torrential rain with gusts of wind strong enough to knock someone over.

Figure 9.1 Kevin and myself somewhere in the Dublin mountains.

I was not only exhausted, but soaked and miserable. As we climbed a particularly steep hill, I remember saying to Kevin, "If there is a pub at the top of this hill, to hell with peace, I am stopping and spending the rest of the day there." The next six hours were some of the most uncomfortable I have ever endured. But, at 6:30 p.m. we saw the signpost for Glendalough, our destination. I remember hugging the sign in utter relief. Not long after we reached our hostel and showered, I felt human again.

The next morning, I woke early and decided to take a walk along the lake of Glendalough. The sun was rising, its rays were glistening on the water, and in the background were the ruins of the first monastic site in Ireland dating back to the sixth century. As I looked, something magical happened. I felt a call within me to stop and spend time experiencing this beauty. Time stopped and I was fully present, in the moment. As I sat there, I was in awe of this amazing display before me. I felt alone and yet connected, disoriented and yet at home. The misery of the previous day faded as my heart and soul were lifted in delight.

As I entered deeper into the experience, I wondered about the wonderful and terrible events that had happened in this place over the past 1,400 years, and as I did, I was drawn in even more. The calm and peace I felt lifted the worries and burdens that were weighing me down. I could breathe again. That morning, I felt the humble walk for peace was part of the bigger story of this place, and we were connected forever. As I left to return home that day, I knew that this place had a unique presence that had touched me and left me inspired, listened to, and connected.

Figure 9.2 A view of the early monastic ruins in Glendalough, one of my thin places.

Glendalough is a "thin place" or Caol Áit (kwe-ol AITCH) in Gaelic. The term comes from Celtic spirituality and was used to describe certain physical places whose presence had a profound impact on people. The place drew them in and made them feel different. The Celts believed that the veil between heaven and earth was "thin" in these places, thus the name "thin place." This thinness made touching the divine easier.

These places have the power to draw us in from the mundane activities of our routine; we become aware of our place in the bigger story of life and of our interconnectedness with the world and with each other. These places trigger both an inward self-reflection and an outward desire to embrace our unique voice and expand our own presence in the world. The power of these thin places is in their ability to jolt us out of our present reality. We are able to see the world and our situation in a new way and become empowered to return with a new perspective and change of focus.

Ireland is full of thin places. When I go back home to visit family, I always try and spend time in some of them. Some of these are the sites of holy places, such as Glendalough, but others, such as the mysterious woodland path in Coole Park, Co. Galway, are not. All of them, however, invite us into a sacred space, transporting us to a deeper reality. While the Celts may have come up with the term, Ireland certainly does not have a monopoly on these places. Thin places can be found anywhere. Take a few minutes and think of some physical places with deep meaning for you. I am sure that some of them have the power to draw you in and change how you feel. Thin places do not have to be in the middle of stunning scenery. In downtown Washington DC, one of my thin places is the Korean War Memorial. I have been there surrounded by hundreds of tourists and have been totally drawn into a deeper reality, feeling as if I was the only one there.

Figure 9.3 The Korean War Memorial draws you into a place of silence and reflection.

What are the elements of this thin place experience? The first and most important is that time takes on a different dimension; it slows down and we become fully present to our surroundings and to ourselves. Thin places enable us to feel calm even in the midst of busyness.

Second, these places widen our perspective. So often, we view our reality with a narrow focus. Thin places help us widen the lens, see reality, and glimpse the bigger connections we fail to see.

Third, thin places speak to our hearts and souls. At its core, spirituality is about connecting with something that is larger than ourselves. That connection, in turn, drives us inward and outward—inward to discover the values that move us, and outward with greater empathy to connect with others and the world.

I also believe thin places can be more than just physical places. We can be thin places for each other; our very presence can have an impact on another person. When people come in contact with us, we can make them feel as if time has taken on a different dimension by the sheer quality of our presence. Our calmness can offer others a respite in the world of ever greater demands. We can help them see their reality with a wider lens and make connections where they have failed to before this. We can help them connect with their inner values and call them to serve others with greater empathy and compassion.

I just heard a wonderful example of this from my friend Michelle Quigley, who went on vacation to Ireland for the first time. Michelle is of Irish decent and she was very keen to trace some of her relatives during the visit. She knew that her family descendants came from County Mayo, on the west coast of Ireland. One day, she found herself in one of the local pubs and was chatting with the owner. She was remarking about how wonderful the visit had been so far and the only thing that would make it better was if she actually met a relative, no matter how distant. He asked what her last name was, and she mentioned it was Quigley. One of the customers, Joe, who was sitting beside them and had been listening to the conversation said there was a Quigley down the road, and he would be happy to take her by.

Michelle was always one for an adventure. So, she went with Joe to a farmhouse a few miles from the pub. A middle-aged woman, Mary, answered the door and Joe spoke with her. Michelle was soon welcomed in with a smile and invited to the front room for a cup of tea and a chat. Joe said he would be back in a little while. When Joe returned one hour later, Michelle knew all about Mary and her family and vice versa. When they were returning to the pub, Michelle thanked him, but Joe said he was sorry. "Whatever for?" Michelle inquired. "Well I was hoping that you would get a chance to meet Kate Quigley who lived next door, but it seems she was delayed on her way home." Michelle was now curious and asked if Mary who she had spent the past hour not a Quigley. "No, she is a Mary Keane but said she was happy to host you while I looked for Kate."

Michelle suddenly realized that Mary who she had been chatting with for over an hour was not even a Quigley but agreed to entertain her while Joe found out if Kate would be home. She said it was the highlight of her trip. Where else would someone interrupt their day and give so generously of their time to a total stranger? In many ways, Mary had been a thin place for Michelle.

The concept of a thin place can also be very powerful for leaders. What if leaders could be thin places for all those who came into contact with them? What might that look like? Let's examine three main areas:

1. The Notion Of Time

If there is a constant refrain from leaders, it is the underlying feeling of a lack of time. Leaders feel the pressure of having more to do with less time. One of the mantras you commonly hear from business gurus is that the skill leaders must master is doing more with less. I have found, however, that most leaders who hear this mantra roll their eyes, as it is code for cutting costs to the bare minimum and leaves them running around like chickens with their heads cut off. It is not hard to see how this has impacted the quality of their presence.

So often we fall into the temptation that we have to multitask and constantly juggle twenty things at once. Of course, we now know from research that multitasking does not work; in fact, multitasking is not even possible. In reality, our brains just cannot focus on more than more thing at a time. We can fool ourselves into thinking that we are doing two things at once, but in reality, we are quickly moving from one thing to the other. The problem is, between each of these micromovements, we lose some of our attention. This phenomenon results in potentially missing important information. When we are listening to someone on the phone, our brain uses the auditory cortex; however, if we then decide to check our email at the same time, we activate the visual cortex and begin to miss part of what is being said on the call. The National Transportation Safety Board reports that texting while driving is the equivalent of driving with a blood-alcohol level three times the legal limit.[41]

I learned the fallacy of multitasking firsthand when my wonderful bookkeeper called me out on my lack of presence. I used to have a standing meeting with her on Friday mornings. She would give me a report on how things were going. Feeling pressed to get things done I would pull up my email screen. I would listen to her while glancing at the screen to monitor what emails were coming in. I thought I did this masterfully without her even noticing. However, one day she asked if she could be candid with me and went on to say that during these meetings, she felt that she was talking to someone who was not in the room. The multitasking façade had come crumbling down. I, without being aware of it, was being disrespectful, and the lack of my presence was felt.

I decided to rearrange my office after that encounter. I brought in a small round table and any time I had a meeting I went to that table away from my work desk. I once heard someone say, "How do you spell love?" The answer was T.I.M.E. I know that leaders have great limits on their time; but the danger is that this pressure can leak into every encounter. We may only have five minutes to give someone, but we can make those five minutes count with the quality of our presence and engagement. In addition, something magical happens when we are fully present. It is as if we are in one of those amazing thin places. Time begins to stretch. What was only five minutes can be felt by the other person as something totally different.

2. Widen Perspective

One of the central and yet difficult tasks of a leader is to view the big picture and see connections where others are unable make them. I have worked with many leaders coming into leadership for the first time, and this transition can be very painful. Most people are promoted to leadership because they have been successful contributors. They have gotten things done and stood out. Up to this point, success has been easily measured.

Once in leadership, however, success is much harder to define and measure. I remember coaching a new leader who was beginning to regret his decision to accept his new role. He started off his session expressing his frustration. "What did I actually do last week?" he began. "I put out a few fires, but I am not sure if I really got anything done." Herein lies the core of the problem. As a contributor, success can be measured by how many widgets you produced; but a leader's measurement can feel much more nebulous. The temptation is to return to the weeds and to the work which is measurable and comfortable. This tendency leads to them micromanaging others.

Nevertheless, the invitation for leaders is to take time to put a different lens on their viewpoint and expand what they are looking at. To see the bigger picture. To macromanage instead of micromanage. One of the suggestions I make to leaders is to schedule time every week for viewing the big picture and engaging in more strategic thinking. I also suggest even moving to a different office or meeting room, away from the distractions in their office, to make the change to big-picture thinking.

Similarly, it is critical that leaders help others see how their role fits into the bigger picture. Very often, when someone is in the weeds, it is difficult to see how their small role has an impact on the overall mission of the organization. Helping them make that connection gives great meaning to what they do.

3. Connect With Heart And Soul

The importance of spirituality is often forgotten in business. Leaders are correctly wary about thinking of it in terms of denominational faith. However, it is possible to think about spirituality outside of these terms. As previously mentioned, at its core, spirituality is about connecting with something larger than ourselves. This connection involves an inward journey to discover the core values that move us. In the busyness of work, we can forget to take time to reflect on these values and to ask if they are aligning with what we are doing. This reflection is important because when we are not aligned with our deepest values, it's impossible for us to be authentic in what we do.

A few years ago, I was coaching a busy mid-level leader named Jerry. He presented me with a dilemma he was having: balancing work and home life. He went on to explain that the demands of work had been increasing so he had been staying later at work, and as a result, had been missing his six-year-old son's soccer games. He felt bad about missing his son's games, but he felt trapped at work.

As we began to explore his core values and what drove him, he was able to realize that at the top of the pyramid was his family and his desire to be present for his children when they were growing up. One session he told me, "I went to the park to reflect the other day, and I realized that in ten years' time when I look back, I am going to feel prouder of the time I spend with my son than of the extra time I spent at work."

Jerry's insight was not easy to put into action. There was considerable pressure on him to stay late at work. However, he also realized that he was working long hours, often getting there at 7 a.m., so leaving work at 4:30 p.m. every once in a while, should not have been a big deal. When the next game came around, he decided to leave despite the looks his peers gave him. The impact of his action surprised Jerry. He told me that during the next week, his colleagues came and thanked him for reminding them what was really important, giving them the impetus to do the same.

We all have thin places in our lives. When we go there, we begin to feel different. What if we might be a thin place for people who come into contact with us? What if the quality of our presence and attention made them feel connected and heard in a powerful way? What if our ability to see the wider perspective helped them see the bigger picture and make connections where they had failed to see them before? What if our attention to living from our deepest values invited them to explore and do the same? This is the type of leadership presence the world is craving.

Lesson 7 Inventory

Reflect on the statement and how you typically "show up" at work. Think of examples in your experience. Place an "X" along the continuum that best reflects you.

I get easily distracted when I am in conversation with another person.	Almost Never True	Almost Always True
I have a sense of gratitude and thanksgiving in life.	Almost Never True	Almost Always True
I am able to make decisions according to my purpose in life.	Almost Never True	Almost Always True
I can quickly see complex problems.	Almost Never True	Almost Always True

Lesson 7 Toolbox

Please visit www.leadershiplessonsfromthepub.com/toolbox

1. Mind Mapping (Worksheet).
2. Values Exercise (Activity).
3. Gratitude Meditation (Activity).
4. How To Be More Present In Conversation (Video).

CHAPTER 10

SLÁINTE

If you spend enough time in Irish pubs, you will hear a word time and time again: sláinte (pronounced a bit like SLAN-che). It derives from the old Irish word *slán*, meaning "healthy, whole or safe." It's the Irish form of cheers, but much richer. It expresses the wish that the other person be healthy, whole, and safe.

Pubs are full of a rich array of toasts and sayings that contain much wisdom and wit. I can remember a few customers had their own favorites they loved to use time and time again. John was great at coaxing another drink out of someone in the pub. He used to say, "A bird never flew on one wing," meaning one drink was not enough, and he was in need of another, preferably bought by another person. When he succeeded, he was gleefully toast them by saying, "May you die in bed at ninety-five, shot by a jealous spouse."

Seamus' toast was short and to the point: "Here's to your enemies' enemies!" Seamus would also be amused by people who would announce that there were leaving and going home and yet be still there two hours later. He loved to say, "If that man went to a wedding, he'd stay for the christening."

Other toasts and sayings I heard over the years, however, summarize the wisdom and lessons drawn from them I have tried to encapsulate in the previous chapters.

Be Sure To Taste Your Words Before You Spit Them Out. This saying reminds us that our words have great power and can set the tone. Therefore, we need to think about the impact they might have before we speak. The leader has great power to set the tone; this tone sends ripples throughout the organization. It's a power, however, often neglected because of its invisibility. Words should be deliberately chosen each and every day.

The saying also points out the ability to slow down between being triggered and reacting to that trigger; to add more choices to how we react. This act of choosing, of course, takes time and practice. It's the invitation to become more self-aware, know what triggers you and the signs that show up in your body, and then from that, introduce more choice in how you react.

LESSON #1: *You Get To Set The Tone* **And**

LESSON #2: *You Have The Power To Choose Your Response Even When You Are Triggered*

Two People Shorten The Road. This little piece of wisdom reminds us that life is better with the company of others. Leadership is a journey in which we take people along with us on the road. This requires the ability to create an experience where they feel connected, listened to, and empowered. This requires a leader to have enough empathy, the raw ingredient of connection.

The saying also reminds us that the journey can be lonely without a companion along the way. Leadership can be lonely; it is critical to have a trusted mentor or a coach, someone who is able to offer advice and counsel, and who is able to help a leader see themselves and others clearly.

LESSON #3: *You Have The Power To Build Community*

Time Is A Great Storyteller. The longer we live, the more experiences we have in life and the more opportunities we have to draw out the stories that come from them. Humans were storytellers long before we could read and write. Story was our language, and it still has tremendous power to connect and engage others in a way that no other medium can.

So many leaders do not realize they possess this vault of gold. The time they've spent in their leadership roles and with their organizations have given them the potential to be great storytellers. Those who do mine this treasure are able to take others on an emotional journey and experience.

LESSON #4: *You Are Called To Be A Seanchaí (Storyteller)*

Do Not Break Your Shin On A Stool That Is Not In Your Way. This saying warns against looking for conflict in places you need not. We all have a conflict story; it shows up in how we approach conflict. For some, we rush in, get involved too quickly, and end up exacerbating the problem. Others, of course, choose not to get involved and resist, which can equally exacerbate a problem.

Managing conflict requires balance. It involves knowing when to engage. It also involves the ability to listen and keep engaged, while at the same time managing your own emotions and triggers. These are essential skills for a leader. Conflict can be a healthy debate or can embody a step over the line and become destructive and petty. The leader is called to steer others toward the former and recover when they do step over the line. Most of all, the leader needs to help build bridges, especially when others cannot see a way past what divides them.

LESSON #5: *You Are Called To Be A Bridge, Not A Wall*

A Good Laugh And A Long Sleep Are The Two Best Cures For Anything. This saying is as old as the hills, yet the wisdom within is being vindicated by discoveries in neuroscience. People who have higher levels of optimism and are able to reframe situations with laughter show higher levels of resilience. During the recent COVID-19 outbreak, my phone would have five to six text messages from my sisters in Ireland with jokes, memes, or humorous videos of their shared locked down experience. It's a trait that runs deep with the Irish.

We also know the importance of sleep and how it supports our ability to be more self-aware and manage our emotions as they arise. There is a direct correlation between lack of sleep and responding in a more reactive manner.

Leaders know the important of resilience and how it can help an organization weather whatever challenges it encounters. The skills of reframing situations with humor and injecting optimism are key ingredients in resilience. Getting enough sleep only sharpens those skills.

LESSON #6: *You Are Called To Hold Space*

God Made Time, But Man Made Haste. One of the most common reactions many visitors to Ireland have is that time seems to slow down. Life in many parts is lived at a different pace, and a premium is put on allotting enough time for friends. What great wisdom for a world that seems to be getting faster by the day! This slower pace has many impacts, but perhaps the greatest is the quality of our presence. The experience between someone who is fully present with you and listening intently, and someone who is there but thinking of the next thing, is cavernous.

A key leadership task is to be more aware of the quality of one's presence in every encounter. It does not mean that one has to spend long amounts of time with everything—a leader does not have extra time. However, when another person encounters a leader who is totally engaged and fully present, even for a few minutes, it can magically stretch time and the felt experience is qualitatively different.

LESSON #7: You have the power to be a thin place

Putting It All Together

What might it look like if a leader were to expand their emotional intelligence and incorporate some of these seven lessons? Let me give you an example. I worked with a client a few years ago—let's call her Sheila—and one of the things Sheila wanted was to really work on expanding her emotional intelligence. In the first few months, we focused on the key areas of becoming more self-aware, becoming more aware of others, managing her emotions, reading other's emotions, and then bringing it together in managing relationships. We incorporated some of the same exercises I have laid out for you in this book.

At the beginning of one session, she came in with a huge smile on her face and said, "I think I nailed it!" She talked about a project that had to be delivered with a really tight deadline, and how everyone was feeling stressed by it. She had a meeting one afternoon and knew that it would be particularly tense because the deadline was looming. Before she left for the meeting, she took some time to check in with herself. She became more self-aware. She noticed that she was carrying a lot of tension and was feeling a lot of anxiety. The last thing she wanted was to say something that she might regret or pass on some of her anxiety (self-awareness).

So, she thought of one of her practices, took deep breaths, and visualized what the meeting would look like. She visualized calming people in the midst of their anxiety and dealing with whatever pressures came up with grace. With that, she stepped away and went into the meeting (self-management).

The minute she went into the meeting, she could feel the tension in the air (social awareness). As she sat down, she recognized what was happening and said, "Look, I know everyone is under a lot of pressure, but I'm sure as a team, we can really pull through." One by one, each person made their report, then it came to Tom.

Now, Tom had a history with Sheila of not delivering when it counted, and lo and behold, today was no different. Tom said, "You know, I've had so many things on my plate, I really haven't quite finished what I meant to." Sheila could feel tension rising within her (self-awareness). She had been triggered, as she usually was by Tom, but was aware Tom was one of her triggers (self-awareness). This time, she had a tool to turn to in the moment of being triggered (self-management). So, instead of saying something to Tom that she would later regret, she stopped, took a breath, and turned to another tool: questions (social interaction).

She turned to Tom and asked, "Tom, tell me, is there anything we need to know about your part of the project?" Tom talked about something that had suddenly come up of which the team had not been aware. Sheila's ability to ask a question in the moment, rather than criticize Tom, helped the team become aware of something they needed to deal with before the project's final delivery. The meeting ended, and three days later, the project was finished on time. Now that's emotional intelligence.

Watch Me Build Again

My father died on August 24, 2000. I was still a priest and returned to Ireland for the funeral in which I was celebrant of the mass. It was one of the most difficult things I have ever done. In the sermon, I quoted a few lines from one of my favorite Irish poets, the late John Donoghue.[42]

FOR A FATHER

The longer we live,

The more of your presence

We find, laid down,

Weave upon weave

Within our lives.

The quiet constancy of your gentleness

Drew no attention to itself,

Yet filled our home

With a climate of kindness

Where each mind felt free

To seek its own direction.

Your presence was a sheltering tree

Where our fledgling hearts could rest.

Something in you loved to inquire

In the neighborhood of air,

Searching its transparent rooms

For the fallen glances of God

These beautiful words evoked the spirit of my father. They also evoked some of the elements of what makes a leader impactful— the power of presence to create a space where others feel safe; the awareness to set a tone that enables other to reach their potential; the ability to be curious and to ask great questions.

A few weeks after the funeral, there was a knock at the door. It was Jimmy, one of our neighbors. "How are you doing, Irvine?" I replied, "Sure, I am OK, Jimmy, considering everything." Jimmy handed me a hammer. "Listen, Irvine, I borrowed this from your daddy and sure, I forgot to give it back to him."

In my hand was a hammer, but in my head were my father's words, "Watch me build again." As I closed my eyes, I felt his calm presence and was reminded of his power within me.

Each and every day we have an invitation to build again. What we build will largely be determined by the emotional skills we have developed from within. Leadership is a noble calling that requires courage. Yet, our world depends on it and is craving leaders who can create spaces that enable us to thrive and be our best selves. May your presence be a gift to others today and every day.

Sláinte

ACKNOWLEDGMENTS

This book has been in my heart and mind for many years. In conversation with so many people after they'd get a flavor of my background, they would tell me I needed to write a book. It's one thing to have the idea inside of you, and another to bring it to fruition. I am indebted to the encouragement and help of so many people.

To my amazing family: This book required me to revisit many painful moments in my family's life. Yet it also helped me see the remarkable example and sheer courage and determination of my parents, Brian and Teresa. They molded a family full of joy and love. In looking at the lives of my sisters, Susan, Ann, Kate, and Mary, it's easy to see the apple did not fall far from the tree, as your lives are also reflections of that same courage and determination.

To my clients who have shared with me their hopes, dreams, and fears: I am in awe of your desire to grow and lead with passion and compassion. This book is an attempt to offer some insights into your struggles as well as some tools to continue your growth.

To my devoted husband, Fred, for your belief in me and constant encouragement: When I went to my first training engagement many years ago, you placed a card in my suitcase which I still have. In the card, you predicted great things for me in the future. In these intervening years, it has become clearer to me, now more than ever, that you are one of those great things that happened to me.

To Henry DeVries and the team at Indie Books International: Thank you for your guidance, encouragement, brilliant ideas, and humor to help make this book a reality.

To Laura and Toni: For your willingness to give the gift of your time to review and critique the manuscript. This is a better book because of you.

To my Salon Group—Joanie, Colin, Linda, Jan, and Dan: For creating a sacred space for me to face some of the fears that have held me back.

To Darren who was so enthused at the idea of *Leadership Lessons From The Pub* that he gave me the initial encouragement to pursue it. To Pam who so loved the idea of a keynote covering this topic, that she booked me for my first engagement with it. She continues to cheer me on.

And finally, to you, my reader: Thank you for taking a risk and gifting me with your precious time to read this book. I hope its stories and insight were helpful to you and those you lead and manage. I offer you an old Irish blessing that I love: *May you get all your wishes but one so you always have something to strive for.*

ABOUT THE AUTHOR

I rvine Nugent believes that leadership development is a journey from the inside out. If our emotional intelligence is lacking, any new business skill we attempt to implement will be adversely impacted. As such, he's spent most of his career helping leaders harness the power of their emotions so they can have deeper connections, make better decisions, and increase their influence.

He possesses fifteen-plus years in senior leadership roles in organizations of various sizes, stages of growth, and sectors. He is experienced in challenging business environments and has worked extensively with emerging leaders as an executive coach and consultant helping them become more self-aware, read the emotions of others, manage their own emotions and relationships.

Born in Northern Ireland, Irvine brings to his audiences a rich and varied experience. Growing up in a society torn apart by division and violence, he saw firsthand the damage done when communication breaks down and people fail to listen and understand. His upbringing inspired him to help leaders build workplaces in which people thrive and realize their full potential.

A gifted storyteller, his programs are infused with passion, dynamism, and of course, his natural Irish humor. Paramount for Irvine is that each person leaves with practical tools based on the latest scientific research that they can implement immediately.

Irvine is an internationally recognized trainer, top-rated keynote speaker, and is one of the few worldwide certified facial action coding system (FACS) coders: Experts in reading facial emotions. He earned his PhD in Management from Capella University with research focused on leadership in times of crisis. He is a graduate of Georgetown University's Executive Coaching Program.

He resides in Washington, DC with his husband, Fred.

For information on speaking and emotional intelligence training please contact Irvine at:

www.irvinenugent.com or irvine@irvinenugent.com.

For additional resources by Irvine Nugent on expanding your emotional intelligence there is an online course available to accompany this book at www.leadershiplessonsfromthepub. com/toolbox as well as weekly YouTube Videos bit.ly/ emotionalintellgience

Connect with Irvine on social media:

bit.ly/emotionalintellgience

linkedin.com/in/irvinenugent

twitter.com/irvinenugent

facebook.com/irvinespeaks

instagram.com/irvine.nugent

ENDNOTES

1 Sarah Campbell. "'We Shall Overcome'? The Good Friday/
   Belfast Agreement and the Memory of the Civil Rights
   Movement." *Open Library of Humanities*, April 24, 2018. doi.
   org/10.16995/olh.259.

2 Thomas Cahill. *How the Irish Saved Civilization: The Untold
   Story of Ireland's Heroic Role from the Fall of Rome to the Rise of
   Medieval Europe.* London: Sceptre, 1995.

3 Cahill, *How the Irish Saved Civilization,* 104.

4 Kevin Martin. "10 Things You Might Not Know About Irish
   Pubs." *The Irish Times*, June 2, 2016. https://www.irishtimes.
   com/culture/books/10-things-you-might-not-know-about-
   irish-pubs-1.2668558.

5 Ray Oldenburg. *The Great Good Place: Cafés, Coffee Shops,
   Bookstores, Bars, Hair Salons, and Other Hangouts at the Heart of
   a Community.* Philadelphia, PA: Da Capo Press, 2005.

6 Daniel Goleman. *Emotional Intelligence: Why It Can Matter
   More Than IQ.* London: Bloomsbury, 2004.

7 Lauren Landry. "Emotional Intelligence in Leadership: Why It's
   Important." Retrieved May 23, 2019, from https://online.hbs.
   edu/blog/post/emotional-intelligence-in-leadership.

8   Dave Infante. "The True Story of How the Irish Ship Entire Pubs Around the World." *Thrillist*, March 13, 2014. https://www.thrillist.com/drink/nation/the-true-story-of-how-the-irish-ship-entire-pubs-around-the-world-thrillist-nation.

9   Dmitry Smirnov, H. Saarimäki, E. Glerean, R. Hari, M. Sams and L. Nummenmaa. "Emotions amplify speaker–listener neural alignment." Retrieved June 2, 2020, from https://onlinelibrary.wiley.com/doi/full/10.1002/hbm.24736.

10   Pavel Goldstein, Irit Weissman-Fogel, Guillaume Dumas, and Simone G. Shamay-Tsoory. "Brain-to-Brain Coupling During Handholding Is Associated With Pain Reduction." *Proceedings of the National Academy of Sciences* 115, no. 11 (2018). https://www.pnas.org /content/115/11/E2528 .

11   Lukas F. Koning and Gerben A. Van Kleef. "How Leaders' Emotional Displays Shape Followers' Organizational Citizenship Behavior." *The Leadership Quarterly* 26, no. 4 (2015): 489–501. https://doi.org/10.1016/j.leaqua.2015.03.001.

12   Mosad Zineldin and Anders Hytter. "Leaders Negative Emotions and Leadership Styles Influencing Subordinates Well-Being." *The International Journal of Human Resource Management* 23, no. 4 (2012): 748–58. https://doi.org/10.108 0/09585192.2011.606114.

13   Nai-Wen Chi, Yen-Yi Chung, and Wei-Chi Tsai. "How Do Happy Leaders Enhance Team Success? The Mediating Roles of Transformational Leadership, Group Affective Tone, and Team Processes." *Journal of Applied Social Psychology* 41, no. 6 (2011): 1421–54. https://psycnet.apa.org/record/2011-13776-007.

14   Daniel Goleman, Richard E. Boyatzis, and Annie McKee. *Primal Leadership: Learning to Lead with Emotional Intelligence.* Boston, MA: Harvard Business School Press., 2013, 27.

15 Thomas Burke and Frederick Carter. *Will Someone Lead Me to a Pub?* London: G. Routledge & Sons, 1936, 42.

16 Douglas Nemecek. "Loneliness and the Workplace: 2020 U.S. Report." *Cigna*, January 2020. https://www.cigna.com/static/www-cigna-com/docs/about-us/newsroom/studies-and-reports/combatting-loneliness/cigna-2020-loneliness-report.pdf.

17 Silvia Marte. "Senior Leaders Are Misunderstanding the Role of Sponsorship—and Missing Out on Its Rewards, According to New Research by the Center for Talent Innovation." *Center for Talent Innovation*, January 18, 2019. https://www.prnewswire.com/news-releases/senior-leaders-are-misunderstanding-the-role-of-sponsorshipand-missing-out-on-its-rewards-according-to-new-research-by-the-center-for-talent-innovation-300774196.html

18 Jacob Guinot, Ricardo Chiva, and Fermín Mallén. "Organizational trust and performance: Is organizational learning capability a missing link?" *Journal of Management & Organization.* May 21, 2014. Retrieved June 2, 2020, from https://doi.org/10.1017/jmo.2014.3.

19 DDI World. "Leadership Skills Research: Insights to Predict Leader Success." https://www.ddiworld.com/hirezleadership.

20 Scott DeRue, Gretchen M. Spreitzer, Brian Flanagan, and Benjamin Allen. "Developing Adaptive Leaders for Turbulent Times: The Michigan Model of Leadership." *European Business Review*, 2013, 57–61.

21 P. Matthijs Bal and Martijn Veltkamp. "How Does Fiction Reading Influence Empathy? An Experimental Investigation on the Role of Emotional Transportation." *PLOS ONE* 8, no. 1 (2013). https://doi.org/10.1371/journal.pone.0055341.

22 Yuan Cao, Luis Contreras-Huerta, Jessica McFadyen, and Ross Cunnington (2015, March 04). "Racial bias in neural response to others' pain is reduced with other-race contact." *ScienceDirect.* Retrieved June 2, 2020, from https://doi.org/10.1016/j.cortex.2015.02.010.

23 Janis Forman. *Storytelling in Business: The Authentic and Fluent Organization.* Stanford, CA: Stanford Business Books, 2013, 6.

24 Antonio Damasio. *Self Comes to Mind: Constructing the Conscious Brain.* New York: Vintage Books, a division of Random House, 2010, 57.

25 Kendall F. Haven. *Story Proof: The Science Behind the Startling Power of Story.* Westport, CT: Libraries Unlimited Incorporated, 2007, 35.

26 Simon Lacey, Randall Stilla, and K. Sathian. "Metaphorically Feeling: Comprehending Textural Metaphors Activates Somatosensory Cortex." *Brain and Language.* Academic Press. February 2, 2012. https://www.sciencedirect.com/science/article/abs/pii/S0093934X12000028?via=ihub.

27 Paul J. Zak. *The Moral Molecule: The Source of Love and Prosperity.* New York, NY: Dutton, 2013, 37.

28 Michael Hauge. *Storytelling Made Easy: Persuade and Transform Your Audiences, Buyers, and Clients—Simply, Quickly, and Profitably.* Oceanside, CA: Indie Books International, LLC, 2017, 21.

29 Jonah Sachs. *Winning the Story Wars: Why Those Who Tell—and Live—the Best Stories Will Rule the Future.* Boston, MA: Harvard Business Review Press, 2012.

30 Howard M. Guttman. "The Leader's Role in Managing Conflict." *Leader to Leader,* 2004, no. 31 (2003): 48–53. https://doi.org/10.1002/ltl.63.

31 *The Way Old Friends Do Words and Music* by Benny Andersson
and Bjorn Ulvaeus. Universal Music Publishing AB, ©1980.
Controlled and administered by Universal–Polygram
International Publishing, Inc. and Emi Waterford Music, Inc.
All rights reserved. Used and reprinted by permission of Hal
Leonard LLC.

32 Laura Riolli, Victor Savicki, and Ariana Cepani. "Resilience in
the Face of Catastrophe: Optimism, Personality, and Coping in
the Kosovo Crisis." *Journal of Applied Social Psychology* 32, no. 8
(2002): 1604–27. https://doi.org/10.1111/j.1559-1816.2002.
tb02765.x.

33 Sofie Vindevogel. "Resilience in the Context of War: a Critical
Analysis of Contemporary Conceptions and Interventions
to Promote Resilience Among War-Affected Children and
Their Surroundings." *Peace and Conflict: Journal of Peace
Psychology* 23, no. 1 (2017): 76–84. https://psycnet.apa.org/
record/2017-05305-010.

34 *It's A Hard Life Wherever You Go* by Nanci Griffith. Irving
Music, Inc. and Ponder Heart Music, ©1989. All rights
controlled and administered by Irving Music, Inc. Used and
reprinted by permission of Hal Leonard, LLC.

35 Rosamund Stone Zander, and Benjamin Zander. *The Art of
Possibility.* Boston, MA: Harvard Business School Press, 2007.

36 Stefanie Mache, Karin Vitzthum, Eileen Wanke, David A. &
Burghard Klapp, and Gerhard Danzer. "Exploring the Impact
Of Resilience, Self-Efficacy, Optimism and Organizational
Resources On Work Engagement." Pubmed.gov, 2014. https://
pubmed.ncbi.nlm.nih.gov/23531578/.

37 Stanford Graduate School of Business. "Laughter: Serious
Business." Video file retrieved from https://www.youtube.com/
watch?v=Nju6yel062Y.

38 Robert R. Provine. *Laughter: A Scientific Investigation.* New York, NY: Penguin Books, 2001.

39 Martin E. P. Seligman. *Learned Optimism: How to Change Your Mind and Your Life.* London: Nicholas Brealey Publishing, 2018.

40 Otto Scharmer and Katrin Kaufer. *Leading From the Emerging Future: From Ego-System to Eco-System Economies.* San Francisco: Berrett-Koehler Publishers, 2013.

41 J.D. Catherine Chase. "U.S. State and Federal Laws Targeting Distracted Driving." *Annals of Advances in Automotive Medicine* 58 (March 2014): 84–98.

42 John O'Donohue. *To Bless the Space Between Us: A Book of Blessings.* New York, NY: Doubleday, 2008.